What people are saying about *The Accidental Sales Manager*

I've known Suzanne Paling for years and am thrilled that her superb work is finally accessible to all. Suzanne has hit a home run! Having helped countless CEOs who found themselves managing salespeople, Suzanne truly speaks from the perspective of a CEO, using case studies anyone in this position can relate to. The clarity and straightforward actions at the end of each chapter makes this a complete and compelling survival guide. I look forward to seeing this in the hands of CEOs, owners, and presidents!

> —Laurie Kirk, CEO,
> The Board Forum CEO Roundtable

Suzanne has been a faculty member at my CEO Boot Camp since 2004 and always delivers engaging and helpful content to the attendees. This book expands on that content, and I highly recommend it for any owner or CEO who is forced to take over the sales management function. And even experienced sales managers will benefit greatly from her wisdom and experience in setting up sales teams to perform. I am sending the manuscript to a client who can't wait for publication.

> —Bob Norton, CEO,
> AirTight Management and
> CEO Coach and Author

Those who are lucky enough to read this book will benefit from the same great advice that I received from Suzanne when I retained her as a consultant. The differences between knowing how to sell and knowing how to manage those who sell is not obvious. Suzanne forced me to focus on what my company really needed, and we ended up with a great sales manager ... and that person wasn't me!

> —Steven Damalas
> President, Electronic Fasteners, Inc.

This is an excellent guide for CEOs to follow in order to expand sales. Suzanne presents the information in a manner that shows her extensive experience in dealing with varying sales and CEO personalities. I would recommend this book to any CEO who is having a difficult time understanding why sales are down or falling short of expectations, regardless of organization size. It is an intriguing look into the dynamic and sometimes perplexing personality of successful salespeople from the viewpoint of CEO.

—Michael Woronka, CEO,
Action Ambulance Service, Inc.

Having worked with Suzanne as a sales management coach for two years, I am excited to have a single reference encompassing her broad sales management expertise. Her easy-to-read style, step-by-step guidance, and numerous checklists, templates, worksheets, and sample letters make it easy to implement her suggestions in a real world environment. As a CEO who still finds himself an "accidental sales manager" from time to time, this book really helps when I need to step in and provide some corrective guidance.

—John Eller, President and CEO
InSight USA

Suzanne Paling offers concrete, practical, and realistic guidance to all of us entrepreneurs who become sales managers by default. We are not trained for this role and need to do it well to be successful entrepreneurs.

I wish I had had this resource for sales management when I started my national 26-year-old, customized online and on-site computer training business. This book is chock full of useful suggestions that have helped me to think of more actions I can take as I strive to be the most successful sales manager possible. Thank you Suzanne!

—Elizabeth W. Brown,
President, Softeach, Inc.

The Accidental Sales Manager

Suzanne M. Paling
Sales Management Services

Entrepreneur
Press

Publisher: Jere Calmes
Cover Design: AndrewWelyczko, CWL Publishing Enterprises, Inc.
Editorial and Production Services: CWL Publishing Enterprises, Inc.,
Madison, Wisconsin, www.cwlpub.com

This publication is designed to provide accurate and authoritative information in regard to the subject matter covered. It is sold with the understanding that the publisher is not engaged in rendering legal, accounting, or
other professional services. If legal advice or other expert assistance is
required, the services of a competent professional person should be sought.
—From a Declaration of Principles jointly adopted by a
Committee of the American Bar Association and
a Committee of Publishers and Associations

ISBN 13: 978-1-59918-398-5
      10: 1-59918-398-6

Library of Congress Cataloging-in-Publication Data
Paling, Suzanne.
  The accidental sales manager / by Suzanne Paling.
    p. cm.
  ISBN 978-1-59918-398-5 (alk. paper)
  1. Sales management. I. Title.
  HF5438.4.P343 2010

                              658.8'102—dc22

Printed in U.S.A.

18 17 16   10 9 8 7 6 5 4 3 2

For Jim

Contents

Preface

PERHAPS SOMEONE RECOMMENDED THIS BOOK SO YOU BOUGHT IT. MAYBE A colleague lent you his copy. Was the book placed on your desk anonymously? Regardless, you now have the book and you really don't want to read it.

As the president or executive of a small company, the responsibility of managing the sales reps fell to you. You don't want the job, but no one in the organization is better qualified to do it. In fact, several valued employees threatened to quit if forced to take on the duties. So you are the sales manager and you're not happy about it.

The whole situation feels uncomfortable. You've never sold anything and have a hard time relating to those who do. Finance or maybe product development—that's where you should be. You feel like managing the sales department is a mistake—an accident if you will.

You need a sales manager to *manage* these salespeople. Someone who will do whatever in the world a sales manager does, like answer the reps' endless questions, make sure they're using the sales software, going out with them on sales calls, and basically, well, keeping them away from you so you can run the company.

But that's for another day because right now you simply cannot afford a sales manager's salary. Budgets are too tight. Unfortunately, your managing the sales staff remains the most sensible and economical plan.

I empathize with how you feel. I work with company presidents like you all the time. It's OK *not* to be excited about being the sales manager. Effective sales managers have a specialized skill set. It's no different from being a plumber or a CPA. You need the right experience, tools, and education to do the job successfully.

Most career sales managers spend years in sales. They understand what the job entails before they accept the position and have many of the competencies needed to succeed. Your training, education, interest, and experience probably lie elsewhere.

Capably managing one or more salespeople has much to do with whether they are right for sales to begin with. Some of it depends on the quality of the training and orientation they receive when they first join the company. Sales representatives who enjoy success from the start are a good fit for the position. They receive the tools necessary to get the job done *before they go on their first sales call.*

Wonderful, you say. That's great for a large company with deep pockets and a separate training department. I don't know how to create an orientation program for a new hire. No one at my company has any expertise in sales. None of us know what to do. And where would we find the time anyway?

For now, you wear the sales management hat at your organization. The success of your business depends on sales. You need to hire, train, and effectively manage the sales force, even on a limited budget. Providing insufficient training and support will *cost* you money and limit the growth of your business. A well-thought-out orientation program helps a company president, even one with no prior sales experience, better manage sales representatives throughout their tenure with the company.

The Accidental Sales Manager reaches out to those presidents, business owners, and entrepreneurs in a small business environment who are surprised to find themselves managing the sales function. Written in language the non-sales business professional can understand, it provides you, the busy company leader, with the encouragement, advice, and tools to successfully introduce new salespeople into your organization without costing a fortune. This strong beginning will help you create a high functioning sales department, even if you have doubts about your ability to do so.

Good luck. Let's get started.

ACKNOWLEDGMENTS

I would like to thank the following people for their help and support throughout the writing and publishing of this book:

- Dr. Bruce Katcher of Discovery Surveys, Inc.
- Michael and Patricia Snell of the Snell Literary Agency
- Mark Campbell of MJ Campbell Associates
- Cliff Hakim of Rethinking Work
- JR Riley
- John Woods and his team at CWL Publishing Enterprises
- Jere Calmes, Leanne Harvey, and Jillian McTigue of Entrepreneur Press

Two clients have made a big impact on this book and on my consulting practice:

- Gary Levine, CEO, Two Step Software. My first client. Thank you for allowing me to do my work without interference and prove to myself that there was a "real business" in what I was trying to do.
- Steve Damalas, president, Electronic Fasteners, Inc. I knew nothing about family businesses before I worked with you and everyone at EFI. Thank you for being so open and honest about the advantages and difficulties involved in running a family business.

Mom, Dad, Carole, and Steve: Thanks for your support throughout all phases of my life.

Alex and Rachel: Your enthusiasm and encouragement meant everything to me as I wrote this book, especially during the difficult days. Set goals. Dream big. Dad and I will be there for you every step of the way.

ABOUT THE AUTHOR

Principal of Sales Management Services, Suzanne Paling has more than 20 years of experience in sales, sales management, and sales consulting for both field and inside sales organizations. Suzanne founded Sales Management Services in 1998 to provide practical advice to business executives, owners, and entrepreneurs seeking to increase their revenue and improve their sales organization's performance.

The Accidental
Sales Manager

Part One

Preparing for the New Hire

Understanding Sales Management in Small Companies

Geoffrey watches the salespeople leave the conference room after another unproductive staff meeting. He suspects that their productivity is low and finds their sales forecasts to be unrealistic. Yet when he questions them about how they spend their time or why a certain account has remained on the forecast for months, they get defensive. Geoffrey would like to be an effective and motivating sales manager, but he lacks a sales background and doesn't always know what to do. Because no one else in the organization could do the job, as company president he has to manage sales.

GEOFFREY'S EXPERIENCE IN THE SALES MEETING CAPTURES THE FRUSTRA-tion many presidents of small companies experience when attempting to manage salespeople. Geoffrey and his business partner's story further demonstrate how many presidents stumble into managing the sales force.

Geoffrey and Helen met as newly minted CPAs working in the construction division of a major accounting firm. As a happy coincidence, each was an amateur computer programmer. Both found the construction industry interesting. During their off hours, they worked together to create a software program that met the unique accounting needs of construction companies.

Using money from their 401(k)s, they left the accounting firm and started their own company. Geoffrey was able to convince four of his former clients to try the software program free of charge for one year. Helen worked on the product development, marketing, and contracts side of the business. Geoffrey, the more outgoing of the two, agreed to be the "salesman" and customer service representative. He would serve as president and Helen as vice president.

The business partners learned during the early years of the company that leveraging prior professional relationships was very different from trying to close a sale with a company where they had no personal contacts. Geoffrey discovered that he was unfamiliar with and really disliked the sales process. To significantly increase revenue, both knew they needed to hire a professional salesperson—an undertaking neither knew anything about.

> **In most small companies the president or owner/operator takes on the role of sales manager. Throughout the book, this person may be referred to as president, business executive, owner, entrepreneur, or sales manager.**

Their desire to increase revenue overrode their fears and they moved forward with hiring a salesperson. The first two hires proved disastrous and on the third try they hired a sales representative both felt they could "live with." Over time, their client roster increased steadily. They began to hire additional personnel, outgrew Helen's basement, and moved into "grown-up" office space, as she referred to it. Today, they are a company of 15 employees (four salespeople) with revenue of $6 million.

Geoffrey and Helen would like to grow the company to $10 million dollars and they know that most of that growth will come through sales. With the exception of one superstar who regularly achieves her sales goals while being a pain to deal with, the current sales staff is neither well-managed nor motivated. They continuously complain that the sales quotas Geoffrey sets are unrealistic. With no experience setting goals, he doesn't know if their complaints are valid or not. He's certain of only two things: the sales reps rarely achieve quota and they don't respect him.

Watching Geoffrey try to run the sales organization causes Helen pain, guilt, and angst. The sales staff intimidates him and he resents having to manage them. Efforts on Helen's part to help him do a better job always result in Geoffrey snarling, "Why don't you manage them then?" Truthfully, she would sooner sell her half of the company and go elsewhere before managing the salesforce herself. She's learned to keep quiet.

Both Geoffrey and Helen are educated professionals who know they need help with the sales force, but their attempts to bolster their skills in this area have been less than satisfactory. They took an expensive sales training course alongside their sales staff but that didn't help Geoffrey manage the group any better. Worried about looking foolish around a bunch of experienced sales managers, he refuses to sign up for any sales management seminars. Books a friend lent him on sales management, with all their charts, forms, and to do lists overwhelm him. Neither he nor Helen know exactly what to do.

Like Geoffrey, owners of small businesses experience a great deal of frustration when interacting with sales. Many manage employees in other departments very effectively. They feel confused when those basic management principals come up short with sales reps. Others wonder why they enjoy managing the production team but don't feel confident when supervising the sales staff.

There are those company presidents who simply cannot believe that someone of their intelligence and expertise "can't get this sales thing right." If they could design a software program, why can't they manage a few salespeople? No matter the situation, if they perceive that they are failing with the sales staff, they devote a greater percentage of time to other departments.

Commonly, business owners react angrily to the situation: "Salespeople are impossible, nothing but big babies. I can't deal with any of them." Others react with blame, feeling they have the potential to be excellent sales managers once they find the "right" salesperson. They hire and fire one rep after another, which proves both demoralizing and expensive. Regardless of which scenario occurs, weak sales revenue and possible business failure may result.

Before outlining the steps involved in helping presidents feel more in control of sales through the creation of a meaningful sales orientation program, I thought I would first review the variety of ways smaller companies might handle what passes as new hire orientation. Though the task often falls to the company president, it can also be foisted off on a human resource professional or a sales "buddy." Occasionally, small companies employ sales managers—but even they may struggle with the new hire, as well.

THE COMPANY PRESIDENT

At the majority of small companies, the president morphs into the sales manager. Most use whatever general management skills they possess and do the best job they can with the sales department. Any true "selling" experience they have might be limited to making presentations or networking with high-level executives like themselves. When sales representatives experience difficulties, they don't have the training or hard sales skills to coach or mentor them.

Few have any idea how to structure the initial first few weeks of the new salesperson's employment. If they plan any kind of orientation at all, it usually involves having the salesperson work with and observe some of their fellow salespeople. Neither the new hire nor the tenured sales rep has any kind of agenda for the time they spend together.

Rarely, if ever, does the president proactively schedule meetings with the new hire. Unless they make an effort to try and speak with the president, most new salespeople spend little time with them. Many presidents express surprise and resentment about the amount of attention the new salesperson seems to need.

Once they feel the new hire is "all set," the president begins to concentrate on other matters. New hires become hesitant to annoy them with yet another question. They start managing their own time and become increasingly independent of the president. The president begins to lose touch with the new hire's day-to-day activities. Despite good intentions on both sides, frustration and disappointment set in.

THE SALES BUDDY

Economical and efficient, the "buddy" sales training methodology has been in existence in the sales world for a long time. New hires are paired with a sales representatives who have been with the company for a while. The two usually work together for a few days.

On the plus side, this system allows new sales reps to listen in on or observe the more senior staff members as they call on clients or give live product demonstrations. New sales reps have an opportunity to work with and learn from someone who actually does the job they will be doing. Bonding and camaraderie can take place. When new reps ask a question of experienced sales representatives, they provide the answer in "sales-ese" (not giving an answer with unnecessary depth).

On the negative side, the senior salesperson has a quota to make and may fit the new hire in as the schedule allows. Some resent being asked to take on any training duties at all and do a so-so job of it. Worse still, if senior salespeople tend to be excuse-makers, they may see an opportunity to avoid making their quota. How could they possibly be expected to realize their sales goals with all of the added responsibility of training a new rep?

With the buddy methodology, the new hire learns how one salesperson does the job. New reps will come away from the training experience looking at their responsibilities from that salesperson's point of view. That's not all bad. But the senior salesperson may have a few habits you don't want passed on to the new hire. As president, you may want new hires to experience a broader view of the company that working with only one or two sales representatives may not achieve.

Current sales staff members should play a big part in new hire orientation. They have a great deal to offer. Not knowing what else to do, many presidents mistakenly rely on the buddy system as almost the entire orientation program. Most new hires emerge from this training methodology with incomplete product and company knowledge.

HUMAN RESOURCES

Given their own busy schedule and limited budget, many well-meaning presidents turn orientation over to human resources. They may feel that the manager is a natural at welcoming new employees.

Human resource professionals usually do have experience with organizing new hire orientation. They understand the benefits for all employees of having a strong introduction to their new employer. Most work closely with senior managers and are not shy about asking them to select someone on their staff to spend some time with new employees. Intuitive by nature, many have a sense of whether someone fits in from a cultural standpoint.

Few human resource professionals have a sales background. Though adept at facilitating the orientation process, most lack the experience to know what the new salesperson needs to learn to be successful. New hires may come away from an orientation organized by human resources with a strong sense of the new company but a weaker sense of their sales responsibilities.

Like the sales staff, human resources should definitely participate in—and in some cases coordinate—new hire orientation. They bring tremendous value to the process. They just shouldn't have to bear responsibility for the entire program.

THE SALES MANAGER

Some small companies hire a sales manager or selling sales manager to run the sales force. With prior sales experience, these managers have a built-in advantage over the company president when it comes to actually selecting and leading the sales force.

All of them remember the difficulties of the first few months on the job. They've been there themselves. They understand the anxiety of the first few sales calls and the early frustrating lack of product knowledge. They know about the embarrassment of fumbling with unfamiliar paperwork or online forms. They've experienced the acute pain of being rejected by a prospect when their pipeline has little in it to begin with.

Despite this familiarity, however, they too often struggle with planning and executing an orientation for the new hire. As sales representatives, many were probably handed the keys to the company car along with a map and some old files (if they were lucky) and told to "get out there and sell." They doubtless spent weeks driving around their territory, getting lost (actually or metaphorically), learning the new product line, and calling company headquarters for answers to questions.

Eventually, maybe their second or third time through the territory, they got their act together and started to really sell. Though they understand how much they would have benefited from participating in one, a formalized training program is sort of anathema to them. They have never seen or been through any type of orientation.

Other sales managers experience the reverse. They began their sales career with large organizations that provided in-depth, multi-week, off-site, highly structured sales and product training. These managers now find themselves working for a smaller organization. Though they value the great training they received, they don't know how to duplicate it, from a time or financial perspective, on a smaller scale.

Whether they attended a well-run new hire sales orientation program or received no training of any kind, sales managers understand the value of such programs. Wanting to sponsor some type of new hire orientation often proves problematic. In a small company, they may find themselves in the difficult position of having to "sell" the idea of an orientation period for their new hires. If owners or presidents aren't "pro-sales" or the company lacks a strong sales culture, they may not understand or support this undertaking. The sales manager's attempts to create an orientation program go nowhere.

THE POLITICS OF ORIENTATION

Company presidents know that while the new sales hires participate in an orientation program, they won't be selling anything. Many find this idea threatening. Convincing other departments to participate in the orientation or convincing an executive committee to buy into the fact that the new hires won't be producing for a time might prove too uncomfortable. This brings many orientation programs to a halt before anyone at the company has a chance to put one together.

In all cases, however, whether due to politics, time constraints, or talent, the person charged with sales management may not be particularly adept at new hire orientation. The person adept at new hire orientation may not have any sales management experience. Many well meaning professionals drop the ball when it comes to having a plan for the initial weeks and months of the new hire's tenure.

All companies need to create a meaningful new hire orientation. Virtually every employee should participate on some level. Because, as I'll discuss throughout the book, the entire company benefits from a well-trained, high producing sales staff.

Many presidents fear that the entire new hire orientation program will fall exclusively to them. Orientation should be a team effort. Presidents, if serving as sales managers, don't need to conduct the entire orientation. They do need to support, organize, oversee, and ultimately take responsibility for the program. The growth of the company depends on it.

2

Organizing the Sales Department

Gretchen opens the envelope and looks inside. Paper-clipped to the bundle of papers she finds a handwritten note from the president. She smiles as she reads it. What a nice personal touch. Underneath the note she finds a more formal letter welcoming her to the company and reviewing some of the basic policies and procedures.

She also sees a copy of the orientation schedule for her first three weeks on the job. Other than lunch and a few breaks, it looks as if she'll be busy. The idea of being well-trained before starting to sell gives Gretchen a sense of security She will be working for a company that invests in the sales staff's success.

Last but not least, she sees the compensation plan, which she studies intently. She knows how much she wants to make in her first year and starts thinking about how many sales she needs to make to earn that kind of money.

Gretchen feels eager to get started. Monday cannot come fast enough.

I STRONGLY BELIEVE THAT THE TRUE START OF THE NEW HIRE SALES ORIENTATION begins not on the new salesperson's first day of employment, but during the interview process. Different companies have different interview practices. Some start with a phone interview and others begin with a face-to-face meeting.

>
> **Whether your company begins with a phone or in-person interview, the focus of the first few meetings should largely be on the candidate's previous experience, skill set, and ability to be successful in your company's open sales position.**

When sales candidates demonstrate that they have what it takes to achieve their sales goals at your company, the focal point of the interview changes. You can begin to talk about what your company has to offer and the expectations that your organization has of its salespeople. Once the expectation discussion begins, the sales orientation process has begun, as well.

Discussing the sales orientation period should include showing candidates where they will sit and giving them a copy of a sample orientation schedule. Reviewing expectations involves letting them take a look at the 30-60-90-day performance reviews and discussing minimum productivity requirements. To have those conversations, all necessary materials must be prepared *well in advance* of the new hire's start date.

The checklist below gives you an idea of what should be completed before the interview process begins:

- Offer letter
- Compensation plan
- Orientation schedule
- Sales toolkit
- Productivity goals
- Sales reporting
- Top accounts
- Pre-employment assessments/sales skills training
- Sales contests
- Performance reviews

Why, you ask, must all of this be done prior to the new salesperson's first day of work? Won't they be spending those early days filling out paperwork and observing the other sales representatives? What's with all the fuss and preparation?

Educating prospective employees about the reality of becoming part of your sales team requires buy-in on their part. To get that buy-in you have to be able to specifically, not generally, articulate the expectations for your salespeople.

This very exercise will scare off any mediocre candidates and get the ambitious ones fired up. Gone are the days in which you hired the best available candidates, kept them around the office for a few days, and then put them on the phone or out in their territory. Now you have a plan in place that will truly support new hires as they learn to be top-producing sales representatives.

Many company presidents feel that their new hires "should already know how to sell" or that "they can learn about the products as they go along." They can only visualize the salesperson sitting around the office all day not selling. They see little value in the orientation process.

Usually, I'm able to persuade my clients that creating an orientation plan is the right thing to do. Having been disappointed with other new hires in the past, they listen. When orientation plans are in place and the president discusses them with the candidates during the interview process, their reactions vary.

A below-average performer will think, "I'd better excuse myself from this interview process. I'll think of something to tell them. This company will track my progress too closely. I won't last long."

An average sales representative will think, "This company holds their sales reps accountable. There are expectations of me from day one and if I can't meet them I probably won't have a job."

A very ambitious, money-motivated salesperson will think, "Wow, I want to work for this company. They have serious expectations and seem committed to investing the time and resources to train me so that I can earn a lot of money. I hope they select me for this position."

When *they* hope *you* offer them the job, candidates see a company with a sales culture. Good things start to happen from there.

> **Surprisingly, when** company presidents see the work involved in the creation of an orientation process, they sometimes realize they aren't ready to hire a sales representative. Many come to the conclusion that it's in their best financial interest to prepare for the new hire first and then begin the hiring process.

WELCOMING THE NEW HIRE

Often overlooked in our casual e-mail and texting era, the offer of employment letter remains a valid tool in the hiring and orientation process. The very act of writing and sending a personalized letter underscores how committed your organization is to the new sales representative's success.

Along with offering details on important issues such as the training salary, target income, health benefits, office hours, and the company 401(k) plan, the letter may also include remarks about:

- Thoughts on why the person is a strong fit for your organization
- Previous successes in the person's sales career
- Other staff members' favorable impressions of the new representative

As for the new hires' workspace during the final interview, show them where they will sit. Take the extra time to make the work area presentable and stock it with basic office supplies. Load their laptop with software a few days before they start. Think about how you would like your workspace to look the first day on the job.

The salesperson will always remember and appreciate these gestures.

COMPLETING AND PRESENTING THE COMPENSATION PLAN

High-performing salespeople have many things in common, money motivation being chief among them. Though a solid market presence, new product offerings, and a strong training program may greatly influence their decision to join your company, the amount of income they will be able to earn outweighs all others.

At many smaller companies, the compensation plan may not be formally written down or is hurriedly being finished during the interview process. Don't make that mistake. Presenting a disorganized or incomplete compensation plan might cause you to lose out on a strong candidate. Write, review, and finalize the plan before the search for a new salesperson begins. Present a finished document to the candidates and discuss it with them in detail during the interview process.

A well-written, well-presented compensation program will reinforce for all candidates that they are making the right decision by signing on with your company. It will motivate selected candidates to learn all that they need to know as quickly as possible so they can start earning a good income.

ESTABLISHING NEW HIRE ORIENTATION

The first few weeks of a sales job are stressful and confusing for most new sales hires. At many companies, after they work with a few of the better sales representatives on staff for a few days, new salespeople are left on their own for long periods of time.

Though they want to start selling and being productive, many are reluctant to just pick up the phone and start calling customers. They may feel that they don't know enough about the product and aren't sure how to go about filling in the gaps in their knowledge. Other new hires are reluctant to ask the busy, harried company president or co-workers for help. Their "orientation" is over, right?

By scheduling each day of the first few weeks for the new salesperson, the manager adds badly needed structure to their early days. This benefits both parties. The pre-planned initial weeks allow new hires to learn what they need to know about the organization and the products or services gradually.

Presidents will know where the new hires are at all times, be able to oversee the amount of time spent with various department managers, and carefully monitor their overall progress. The new salesperson has an organized, cohesive introduction to the new employer. The president gains a better understanding of what the new salesperson may need, going forward, in terms of support and training.

CREATING A SALES TOOLKIT

A lot of company presidents feel that only very large organizations have the budget and staff to create a sales training binder or toolkit. Others feel that sales representatives should arrive at the company knowing how to sell and shouldn't need one. Though your new hires probably have previous sales experience, they have never sold your particular product or service before. They will be unfamiliar with, for example, common customer objections or questions. Having to learn these things on their own takes time and slows them down. Furthermore, having the answers "cookbooked" decreases the likelihood that they will improvise and make a mistake.

By working as a team, any size sales organization can put a budget-friendly training binder together. At minimum, it should contain the following:

- Sample introductions
- Qualifying questions
- Common objections
- Template e-mails
- Interview questions
- Sample closes

During the assembly of your company's toolkit, you might want to include a section or two not included in my list. Ask yourself what type of information you would want to have if you were out there selling. What would give new hires a significant jump-start in accelerating their sales performance? Those two questions will help you decide what type of additional information would complete your toolkit.

ASSEMBLING MARKETING COLLATERAL

Under pressure to memorize a lot of data about the product or service they represent, new sales reps sometimes make mistakes when answering their prospects' questions. Though all new sales representatives make the occasional slip-up, the number of factual mistakes can be minimized by providing them with easy-to-follow and up-to-date marketing collateral.

Marketing materials contain hard data about the company and its products or services, including:

- Product fact sheets
- Competitive fact sheets
- Frequently asked questions
- Sample proposal
- Company history/facts

During the early days with their new company, most new sales reps get tripped up when asked in-depth questions about their product or service. Minimize the problem by including this critical but often-forgotten material as part of the toolkit.

SETTING REALISTIC GOALS

New salespeople rarely perform to the level of a tenured sales representative in the first weeks and months. To avoid putting them under too much pressure, many well-meaning managers assure them that they will not be expected to produce for "a while." Not knowing what "a while" means, the new rep loses focus.

Other sales managers give new hires the same goals as a tenured salesperson, figuring "they will catch up eventually." Those goals, impossible to meet in the near term, prove stressful and distracting for the new hire. Either scenario may result in the new sales representative under producing.

All sales representatives, new or established, need productivity goals to help them focus. Goals for the new hire need to be scaled to reflect their tenure and product knowledge. Using the goals for your current sales staff as a guideline, come up with a set of achievable objectives for a new hire.

If the number of prospecting or cold calls is set at 125 a week for your existing staff, set a target of 40 per week for the new rep. Gradually raise the target each week until the new rep reaches the level of the other reps. In this way, the new hire will feel motivated and challenged rather than confused or uncomfortable.

CALLING ON THE LARGEST ACCOUNTS

All salespeople (except perhaps those at entry level) understand that their largest accounts are often responsible for the majority of the sales revenue in their territory. Some are anxious to "jump right in" and start calling on these accounts, but most will want to wait until they have better product knowledge. They understand the importance of the first meeting.

Sales reps need guidance when it comes to initiating contact with their key accounts. Whether you accompany new salespeople on their first call to a key account or have the salesperson currently handling that account make an introduction, you need to have a plan for the new hires to follow. This should include providing them with reports on:

- Historical sales figures
- Current sales revenue
- Description of the business
- History of the company's relationship with the account

Presidents need to mention whether the customer has received any "special treatment" in the past or had any recent issues with your company. The loss of even a single major account can jeopardize a business's future. The salesperson needs the proper information and coaching before beginning to call on these accounts.

PROVIDING SALES SKILLS TRAINING

Before being offered a position with your company, applicants may be asked to take certain types of pre-employment assessments, such as a personality profile or writing sample. Candidates for sales positions should take those as well as a separate assessment focusing exclusively on sales skills. Despite the potential awkwardness, the results of that assessment should be discussed with them during the interview process.

If the assessment shows weak scores, for example, in the area of qualifying questions or closing, sign them up for some sales training. Make sure it starts shortly after the first day on the job. Your new hire orientation program, no matter how thorough and well-organized, will focus primarily on company and product knowledge, not sales skills. Don't mar new sales representatives' beginning at your company by having them carry some of the same sales problems they had before into the new position.

Be the employer that addresses and attempts to correct some of these issues. The payback is strong. Most new hires appreciate investments in their careers. If they embrace the training, it can significantly improve their earning potential.

Tracking Progress and Performance

Sales reports enable a manager to track how much time salespeople are spending on different sales activities, if they are meeting their productivity goals, and whether their efforts are translating into real sales. In other words, the sales reports paint a picture of the sales representatives' day even when the manager can't be there to observe them.

The information in these reports plays a critical part in helping a manager decide whether a sales representative will be successful with the company. The basic suite of sales reports should include:

- Daily call: the type and number of calls
- Productivity: calls and activities versus goals
- Pipeline: number of prospects in different stages of the sales cycle
- Sales forecast: prospects in final stages of the sales cycle
- Long range sales forecast: prospects who may buy in the future

Sales reports are only as good as the information your new salesperson enters into the sales software system. Therefore, any expectations that you have of the candidate in that regard should be made clear during the interview process. New hires should get into the habit of using the sales software system from day one.

Sponsoring Motivating Sales Contests

Salespeople work very hard before they close a sale. Staying motivated and focused throughout the entire sales process isn't always easy. Sometimes salespeople feel that their efforts go unacknowledged. Sales contests are a great way to recognize and reward a lot of the pre-work that goes into a closed deal.

New hires need sales contests too. No matter how much effort they put in, their first sale might not take place for several months after their first day on the job. Signed contracts and commission checks sometimes seem far away to them.

A wide variety of fun, short sales contests will keep them motivated. Don't make sales revenue the focus in the beginning. The new hire probably isn't selling a whole lot just yet. Think of the sales-based activities that might increase the chances of closing a sale, such as product demonstrations, and then create a few contests with those in mind.

CONDUCTING PERFORMANCE REVIEWS: THE 30-DAY REVIEW

Many presidents believe that "there are few good salespeople available." This leads to their tolerating underperformance or bad behavior from those that they do hire. That shouldn't be so. They can do a lot to prevent any drama from playing out by hiring the salesperson for a 90-day trial period. During this critical period, the president should review the new hire every 30 days.

This whole process begins with a 30-day review. Speaking to new hires formally at the one-month mark will reinforce that they are:

- Being held to the standards discussed in the interview process
- Working for a company with a strong support system that gives them every chance of succeeding
- Reporting to someone who is truly managing the sales effort

Presidents sometimes balk at conducting a 30-day review. Many feel 30 days isn't a long enough period in which to judge a new rep. Once they write the first review, most are surprised at how much there is to talk about—even after just one month. Sales toolkits, formal orientation, and fair and thorough review processes play major roles in creating a pro-sales environment and a strong sales culture.

Conducting Performance Reviews: The 60-Day Review

The 30- and 60-day reviews are very different from on another. In this period, presidents go from making the new salespeople an offer of employment to working with them day-to-day for nearly two months.

The new hires now have a track record from the first 30 days that can be compared with their productivity during the second 30 days. More of their work persona is starting to emerge and they are developing a greater understanding of their new place of employment.

During the 60-day review, discussions will involve whether they have:

- Met the initiatives established at the 30-day review
- Taken their product knowledge to a higher level
- Begun to develop a pipeline of prospects
- Turned in a sales forecasting report with closable deals

  Presidents may also discuss the new hires' ability to:

- Manage their own time
- Work independently
- Take responsibility for their own learning and development
- Demonstrate the ability to succeed at the company

These all-important reviews don't take the place of regular unstructured interactions between the president and the new hire. The president should still drop by to chat with the new rep from time to time. New hires will appreciate and glean a lot of interesting information from these impromptu talks.

Conducting Performance Reviews: The 90-Day Review

During days 30 to 60, new hires are proving that they have the *potential* for success at the new company. From days 61 to 90 they should perform, in all respects, close to the standards of a tenured sales representative.

This should include:

- Achieving 90% or more of productivity goals

- Communicating strong product knowledge
- Having a pipeline with an adequate number of prospects at all stages of the sales cycle
- Closing one or more sales (depending upon the length of the sales cycle)
- Demonstrating familiarity with their customers and their sales territory
- Generating ideas of their own for improving their sales performance

When they have completed the 90-day review, presidents will feel confident in their ability to make an unemotional and fact-based decision as to whether to offer the new hire a full-time position. It dramatically changes their ability to hire and manage salespeople going forward.

OFFERING THE NEW HIRE A FULL-TIME POSITION

Unaccustomed to hiring a salesperson for a probationary period, many company presidents aren't exactly sure how to handle the transition process should they decide to offer the new hire a full-time position. Some simply call the salesperson into their office, give them the good news, and then get on with the day. A lot of the time they're relieved to have made a successful hire and just want to get to the papers piling up on their desk. What a lost opportunity!

After all the hard work that has gone into the hiring and orientation process, make a bigger deal out of it. Take the time to:

- Write a letter of congratulations
- Take the salesperson out to lunch
- Ask other executives at the company to call and congratulate the new salesperson
- Have lunch brought in for the whole sales team

If salespeople work remotely and the budget permits, fly them into the office. If that's too expensive, arrange for a conference call that allows the entire staff to offer congratulations. Do something to commemorate the occasion. Both of you put a lot of hard work into this relationship. Don't make it another humdrum day at the office.

COMPLETING ORIENTATION AND MOVING ON TO THE NEXT PHASE

Perhaps mistakes have been made with new sales representatives in the past, such as managing them too loosely or asking them to make sales calls before they were ready. Maybe there was a period of time when you as president hired a series of average salespeople and were continually disappointed with the results.

This time you made an all-out effort to work closely with the new hire and the results are showing. A strong working relationship exists between the two of you. But time spent with the new sales hires meant putting other initiatives on hold. Don't damage this bond as you scale down the amount of time spent with them.

Presidents are completely justified in looking forward to being more independent of new hires and working on other projects. Just don't revert to the old habit of spending an inadequate amount of time with them. The new hires need to feel confident that even though meetings with the president will be less frequent, they will be held at regular intervals.

Topics to include during future meetings might include:

- Territory coverage
- Account penetration
- Time management

Sales staffs may wonder if changes in presidents' behavior—spending more time with sales issues—will be temporary or permanent. An effective way for you to demonstrate an ongoing commitment to the sales staff involves discussing projects you would like to work on during the current sales year. Those could include:

- Writing formal job descriptions
- Creating a policies and procedures manual
- Designing quarterly performance reviews
- Offering career development opportunities

Let all employees—regardless of which department they're in—know that you're as closely connected to their success as ever. Then live up to the spirit and letter of that statement going forward. It will have a positive effect on the growth of the business for years to come.

3

Welcoming the New Hire

Jonathan was thrilled when the president called and offered him the sales position. Though he enjoyed his current sales job, this was the type of opportunity he had been waiting for. He gave his resignation and worked out a start date with his new company. That was more than a week ago and he hasn't heard from anyone at his future employer since.

He wonders whom he should ask for when he arrives on the first day. What will he be doing? Whom will he be working with? Should he bring a lunch? Is it appropriate to call the company president and ask a few of these questions, or will that look idiotic? Where will his desk be? He forgot to ask these questions at the last interview.

Jonathan wishes he had a little bit more information. He tells himself that company presidents get busy sometimes and that she will, of course, be ready for him on the agreed-on day. He's starting to feel really nervous.

No matter how many times they have exceeded quota, won contests, or made President's Club, all salespeople know, deep down, that their last sale, no matter how large or prestigious, is already history. Not only that, by switching companies they will have to start all over again. On day one with your organization, new sales reps will not have made a single sale. This produces anxiety and questions in their minds. What if I could only sell at my previous company? What if I can't replicate that at my new place of employment?

THE ORIENTATION PACKAGE

Salespeople feel very insecure in the early days of their employment with a new organization. No president can completely change that. Letting new sales reps know that you're totally and thoroughly prepared for their arrival, though, helps to minimize these apprehensions. Sending new sales reps an orientation package prior to their start date gets the employee–employer relationship off to a good start.

This package should contain:

- A letter of welcome
- A copy of the compensation plan
- A two-week itinerary

The letter of welcome (shown on the next page) should be the first item new reps see in the package. It sets the tone for those early weeks. If your organization had a lot of interest in this candidate, chances are a lot of other companies would have welcomed them on their sales staff, as well. Use the letter as a way of reminding sales reps that because of the career opportunities offered, they have made the right decision by choosing your organization.

Be sure to personalize the letter with specific information that relates to the individual just hired.

This letter says that we are excited about YOU coming to work for us—not any salesperson—YOU in particular. It also reinforces the fact that you (the president) are there to support new salespeople in any way you can. They may not have technically started their employment with your organization yet, but they are already a part of it, and you are available to them if need be.

A letter like this means a lot to salespeople. They will show it to

---

The Ridgefield Company
25 Maple Lane
Anywhere, USA 12345

Dear New Hire:

During the interview process you impressed all of us with your extensive knowledge of our industry and a consistent ability to exceed your sales quotas. I am pleased that you accepted the position of Sales Representative at the Ridgefield Company.

Salary
Your first day of work will be on Monday, August 20, 20xx. The starting base training salary will be $55,000 for a period of three months. On November 20, 20xx, the base salary will be $40,000 annually.

Benefits
Ridgefield offers medical, dental, and vision plans through the ABC HMO, and you are eligible for benefits 90 days after your start date. We offer a matching 401(k) plan. Short- and long-term disability as well as life insurance, are electives and available under a separate carrier.

Vacation allotment is 10 paid days per year. In addition, there are two paid personal days and five paid sick days annually.

The Ridgefield Company's office hours are 8:30–5:30 Monday through Friday.

Territory
In the position of sales representative, you will be responsible for all direct sales activity in the Midwest territory of Missouri and Illinois.

Expenses
On the first day of employment you will be issued a laptop and cellular phone. All maintenance and related costs will be the responsibility of The Ridgefield Company. Any additional work-related expenses will be reimbursed after an expense form is submitted.

When you shared your story about the most difficult sale you ever closed, I felt certain that you would make a strong complement to our sales staff. All the sales representatives enjoyed meeting you. Jane Johnstone, in particular, looks forward to having another avid cyclist join the group.

Attached are copies of the compensation plan, as well as your orientation schedule for the first two weeks. Ask for Richard in human resources when you report to the office on Monday. Once your paperwork is completed, you and I will work together and join a few of the salespeople for lunch.

Please call me if you have any questions prior to your start date. I look forward to seeing you on Monday.

Sincerely,

Mary Smith

President

family and friends and comment on it during their first day on the job. Trust me on this. Though a letter will never relieve all of their anxiety, it will give them a surge of positive energy that they need. It will tell them that they are respected for their past accomplishments and welcomed as a valued member of the sales team. Once you have the basic template down, adding the personal touches takes just a few minutes. It's well worth the extra effort.

THE WORK AREA

This may seem obvious, but in my years as a consultant I have many times seen the crestfallen faces of sales representatives as they look at their work area.

New hires often open a desk drawer to find only a few grubby pencils in it. Eager to familiarize themselves with their new laptop, they find that it has no software loaded onto it. They may not have been given a password to access a database. No one has ordered any business cards for them and they have no idea how to set up their voicemail.

The beleaguered president may say to himself, "What's the big deal? They'll be working with the other reps for the first few days anyway. By that time, all the software should be installed on their computer. If they need to make a phone call, they can use their cell." For the new hire though, the lack of an organized workspace has a negative effect on their early days with their new organization.

Why does this scenario occur at all? If most presidents wouldn't even consider bringing the new accountant or marketing director into a shabby, barely functioning office, how do they justify treating a salesperson in this way—especially when a salesperson will be generating revenue that a marketing or finance professional never would?

Like any profession, sales has its long-held beliefs. An old adage says salespeople's offices should never be a comfortable place for them to work. They should have nothing more than the bare essentials such as a plain desk and a beat up chair. Why? Because they should be out on the road selling. If their offices are plush and fully appointed, they will spend their time there rather than in front of customers.

Now this thinking was in vogue long before the personal computer or even the fax machine was commonplace in most offices. Today, the sheer amount of basic equipment needed to function in the modern work environment, the increase in the number of inside sales forces, and the availability of the Internet has changed the whole notion of office space over the last few decades.

What remains of this "don't make them comfortable" mentality means that sales representatives, who will have a major impact on company revenue and overall profitability, are sometimes given the least consideration when it comes to their office spaces.

A checklist of appropriate equipment and supplies for new hires could

> **Give someone in your organization the responsibility for ordering all the necessary equipment and supplies as soon as you decide to hire another salesperson. This individual should make sure that salespeople have as a clean, organized, and functional work area for their first day on the job.**

include the following:

- Business cards
- Office supply store gift certificate
- Desk and chair
- Cubicle walls
- Working phone
- Headset
- Basic office supplies
- Company letterhead/envelopes
- Functional computer
- Keyboard
- Cell phone

DOLLARS AND "SENSE"

Readying new sales representatives' work areas before their first day involves extra effort. A bottom line benefit exists, though. Salespeople who have all the equipment and training they need to do their job, even if they don't actually start selling for a few weeks, get off to a faster start.

Even the most ambitious salespeople will be agitated and behave differently than they might ordinarily without all the proper office equipment and sales materials. For instance, they might avoid making cold calls, since they lack the capability of sending e-brochures or looking up information about the customer.

A faster start means higher-quality sales calls and more prospects in the pipeline—almost right from the beginning. This in turn yields more closed sales.

Most importantly, however, if they don't have their business cards, absolutely everything can grind to a halt. Salespeople hate and detest staring their new position without them. On their first day, place their new business cards right in the middle of their desk. Nothing says "we want you to succeed here" to a new rep like being greeted by that sight. Right next to their business

Order business cards as soon as a candidate accepts the open sales position.

cards place a gift certificate to the local office supply store so that they can make a few purchases of their own. They will remember those gestures, always.

THE VIRTUAL SALES REPRESENTATIVE

Technology now makes it possible for small companies to hire sales representatives to work in territories many hundreds of miles away from the main office. Large companies hired remote sales forces for decades and out of necessity created an infrastructure for managing their sales efforts. When smaller companies hire remotely for the first time, no formalized communication or management system exists.

Before hiring remote salespeople, have a discussion about their current office set-up. They may have been working out of a home office for years and already have much of the necessary equipment. On the other hand, if they've recently resigned from another company, their former employers may have taken it all back. As part of their employment contract, agree upon what the company will provide or buy and how reimbursement will work.

No matter what their inventory of office equipment, remember that your new sales representatives will be working for your company. You have a big say-so in how they conduct business. If the sales rep tells you, for instance, that he or she has had the same cell phone number for years and would like to keep it, that's fine if it works for your company.

If, however, the rep's phone isn't compatible with your organization's technology, the new rep will need to use the cell phone you provide. The same holds true for every other piece of technology such as laptops, fax machines, e-mail, Blackberries, etc.

> **New salespeople are the face (and voice) of your organization.** Everything they do must be consistent with how you want your salespeople to communicate with and represent themselves to your customer base.

Immediately on hiring new remote sales representatives, select someone from your home office to coordinate the set-up of their workspace. The employee should come up with a checklist of items needed for the new hire's office. Make sure all the items are sent, and contract for IT help needed with a local IT provider. The package sent out could include:

- Business cards
- Office supply gift card
- Headset
- Phone system
- Laptop
- Software
- Fax machine
- Cell phone
- Sales toolkit
- Company stationery
- Marketing materials
- Pricing information
- Samples

Sales representatives' offices—wherever they may be located—should be an integral part of their success. When salespeople sit around waiting for the proper equipment, they are not as focused or productive as possible. This costs your organization money. Make the set-up of the rep's office environment as important a part of orientation as any other. It will pay off.

4

Completing and Presenting the Compensation Plan

Cecile can hardly wait to start her new sales job. In her current sales position, she earns approximately $85,000 annually. Her income potential at her new company will be closer to $120,000. During the interview process she met the most senior sales rep at the company. He confirmed that he was earning that much, so Cecile knows the potential exists.

But she does wonder if the other sales representatives make as much money. She didn't get a chance to speak with any of them when she interviewed there. Has the senior sales rep always earned $120,000?

Though she was shown the compensation plan when she met with the president, she doesn't have a copy. When she asked for one, the president mentioned needing to add a few last-minute details that wouldn't change the basic plan itself. Should she have insisted on seeing the final plan before she started? Oh well. Cecile only knows that she cannot wait to start making $120,000. The additional income will make a difference to her lifestyle.

CECILE WILL BEGIN THE FIRST DAY OF HER NEW JOB WITH THE EXPECTATION of earning $120,000 annually. In fact, she and her husband are already planning to redecorate their living room—a project they put off because they felt they couldn't afford it. Though it won't be as much fun as redoing the living room, she looks forward to putting more money into their savings and retirement accounts, as well.

Should Cecile discover, several months into her tenure at her new company, that the earning potential was exaggerated, her relationship with her employer will be negatively impacted. Depending on how much of a gulf exists between what she was promised and what she's likely to earn, she may leave the company as soon as she's secured another position.

A sales candidate like Cecile might be impressed by your office building or look forward to representing the state-of-the-art product your company produces. Perhaps the easy commute from home or a very desirable sales territory factored into her decision to come to work for you. She probably found many facets of the overall job offer attractive. None of the aforementioned, however, trumped her enthusiasm for the compensation plan.

A career in sales comes with unique pressures and difficulties. The ability to earn good money offsets the downsides. Therefore, the compensation plan plays a key role in the hiring process.

Business executives often make mistakes when discussing the compensation plan with a sales candidate, and that has a detrimental effect on the hiring process. Some of those errors include:

- Failing to finalize the plan before the interview process begins
- Over-promising the annual income
- Not being prepared to negotiate certain aspects of the plan with the interviewees
- Altering the plan between the time the offer is extended and the new hire starts
- Neglecting to solicit the opinions of peers and current sales staff

BE REALISTIC, NOT OPTIMISTIC

Anxious to entice good candidates to work for their company, presidents may talk excitedly about income potential, focusing almost exclusively on the highest earnings possible within the compensation plan. Though they mean well and really want the candidate to earn this type of money, there are risks involved in concentrating specifically on top tier pay.

What if only one person on the sales staff earns this type of money? What if this person has been with the company for years and handles many lucrative key accounts? Can a new sales representative realistically earn the same amount? What about a situation in which one sales representative briefly earned that amount of money several years ago but no other salesperson has been able to duplicate that effort since? Should that situation be used as an example for the new hire? What are the true average annual earnings for the sales staff? What if the compensation plan is brand new and untested? Can you really guarantee income of a certain level?

> **While high earnings are possible within your compensation plan, if no one at the company earns that amount routinely, any assurances made to potential candidates during the interview process could cause problems once they become employees**

Seasoned sales veterans will ask questions and uncover the truth about how much money sales representatives at your company actually earn. They may quickly determine that no sales rep earns the high salary you are touting. If this happens, your credibility with them will be damaged and they may remove you from the list of potential employers they are considering.

Less experienced sales representatives will probably take you at your word. When they discover six months later that the earning potential was exaggerated, they will be angry. If they stay with the company, which many will not, they'll remain disgruntled, average producers.

Go ahead and discuss your top salesperson's earnings as a way to show candidates the possibilities within your organization. Get them pumped up. Be sure to balance the equation by talking about the high-earning rep's work ethic, for instance, or accounts the rep has built up over the years.

You may have improved your hiring process and feel that the candidate you are currently interviewing might be a stronger salesperson than anyone on your current staff. Talk about the money you can envision the person making. But be as *specific* as possible about why you think this person can out-earn the other sales representatives.

Avoid having a disgruntled salesperson on staff. Don't make false promises with regard to income. Present the compensation plan with integrity. Round out the conversation by having a realistic discussion about such things as:

- The top salesperson's income progression over the years
- True first-year earnings potential
- Average compensation among the sales staff

During my time as a corporate sales manager I was once asked to manage a group of salespeople in another division. Even though I was staying with the same company, this new sales staff was totally unfamiliar to me. I hadn't hired any of them. I knew none of them personally.

The first staff meeting that I held was an absolute disaster. Among their many, many complaints was the issue of being told in their final interview that their income would easily be $15,000 to $20,000 dollars higher than it was proving to be in reality. They were really angry. Rather than make any attempt to defend or justify what they had been promised with regard to their earning potential I just listened.

This group had a lot of other problems as well, many of which were not their fault. The product line was unwieldy and confusing. One salesperson was particularly disruptive. They did not receive the support and attention from marketing that some of the other sales divisions could count on. When I discussed all of my findings with the vice president of sales, what eventually transpired was a complete reorganization of the line.

This reorganization has always been one of the most interesting and fulfilling projects of my career. A lot of problems got addressed and lucrative incentives were put in place for the sales representatives. Despite all of that, I knew that at least a few of them would never be happy working for the company. They would not be able to get over what they saw as a bait-and-switch tactic where income was concerned.

Many of the salespeople were reassigned, quit, or asked to leave. The whole personnel exercise was depressing, expensive, and in many cases, totally unnecessary. If some of the salespeople had been able to focus on their sales efforts and put the income debacle behind them, I think many could have stayed on at the company and enjoyed their work there. But it wasn't to be for a lot them. I trace it back to early promises about an income that was unrealistic and unattainable.

THE COMPENSATION PLAN

During the interview process, many company presidents communicate the specifics of the compensation plan verbally—often leaving candidates to jot down the details on a pad of paper. The potential problems with this arrangement are many, including interviewees interpreting the plan in their own way based on hastily scribbled notes.

A compensation plan, arguably the most important component in the hiring process, should be presented to the candidates as a finalized and formal document. For this to occur it needs to be prepared and ready before the hiring process begins. A well-written compensation plan should include some of the following:

- Training salary
- Training commissions and/or bonuses (if applicable)
- Permanent base salary
- Commissions and bonuses
- Sales quota
- Examples of payouts
- Policies and procedures

On the next pages is an example of a relatively simple formal compensation plan. Your company's plan may include more complex components such as profit margins and/or renewals payouts. Some of your policies and procedures may vary greatly from what I show here. That's fine. I'm simply presenting a simple version of a finalized compensation plan.

The Ridgefield Company
Sales Compensation Plan
January 1, 20xx – December 31, 20xx

Training Salary/Commission

All sales representatives will receive a training base salary for the first three months of their employment ($55,000 annually/$4,583 monthly). For that same initial three month period a flat 4% commission will be paid on all gross sales revenue starting at dollar one.

Compensation Plan

Base Salary: All full-time sales representatives with 90 or more days of tenure will be paid a base salary of $40,000 annually/$3,333 monthly. The Ridgefield Company does not issue annual base salary increases.

Target Performance: Annual: $1,500,000   Quarterly: $375,000

Commission

$0 – $375,000	4%
$375,001 – $500,000	6%
$500,001+	7%

Quarterly Bonus

$1,000	$375,001–$500,000
$1,500	$500,001 or more

Sales Department Policies

Sales representatives are eligible to participate in the compensation plan after 91 consecutive days as an employee of the company.

All commissions and bonuses for the prior quarter are paid during the first pay period following the last day of the business quarter.

Commissions are based on paid invoices received during the current business quarter.

The salesperson must be employed with the company on the last day of the business quarter to receive any commissions and bonuses due them.

If a territory change occurs, the salesperson will receive all commissions and bonuses due them from both their old and new territory through the end of the quarter.

When a territory change is made, the salesperson will be asked to submit a list of all accounts in the old territory that are closable within 30 days. Once the list is approved, both the current and former salesperson in that territory will receive full commission on the sale. Sales that close on Days 31–60 will result in a split commission between the two parties. Sales closing on day 61 will be fully commissionable to the current sales representative in that territory.

Refunds made to customers for any reason will be deducted from the salesperson's overall sales revenue. Any commission earned as a result of the sale will be deducted, as well. If the value of the refund is greater than $50,000, 50% will be deducted in one business quarter and 50% in the next business quarter.

Failure to be at 90% of quota or to be performing at less than the group average for two consecutive months will result in the salesperson being placed on probation. Being placed on probation more than twice during the year will result in termination.

This plan may be amended, revised, or cancelled at any time during the year. Sales representatives will receive notification of these changes.

Earnings Examples

Training Salary
Example 1

Quarterly Sales:		$75,000
Base Salary	3 mos.	$13,749
Commission	$75,000 x 4%	$3,000
Total Quarterly Pay		**$16,749**

Example 2

Quarterly Sales:		$150,000
Base Salary	3 mos.	$13,749
Commission	$150,000 x 4%	$6,000
Total Quarterly Pay		**$19,749**

Compensation Plan
Example 1

Quarterly Sales:		$375,000
Base Salary (3 mos.)		$10,000
Commission	$375,000 x 4%	$15,000
Bonus		$0
Total Quarterly Compensation		$25,000
Annual Earnings:		**$100,000**

Example 2

Quarterly Sales		$450,000
Base Salary (3 mos.)		$10,000
Commission	$375,000 x 4%	$15,000
Commission	$450,000 X 6%	$4,500
Bonus		$1,000
Total Quarterly Compensation		$30,500
Annual Earnings:		**$122,000**

Example 3

Quarterly Sales		$562,000
Base Salary (3 mos.)		$10,000
Commission	$375,000 x 4%	$15,000
Commission	$125,000 x 6%	$7,500
Commission	$62,000 x 7%	$4,340
Bonus		$1,500
Total Quarterly Compensation		$38,340
Annual Earnings:		**$153,360**

Though I recommend that the compensation plan itself be presented in a straightforward style with no embellishments, you still want the current staff to know how excited you are about it. Convey your enthusiasm and support through a cover letter like the one shown on the next page.

GETTING FEEDBACK

Now that we've outlined the best way to present a compensation plan to a job applicant, let's spend a little time thinking about what

---

The Ridgefield Company
25 Maple Lane
Anywhere, USA 12345

June 10, 20XX

Dear Max:

It is my pleasure to present the new compensation plan for 20XX.

This motivating and financially rewarding compensation plan has unlimited earnings potential based on the achievement of your individual sales targets. Your commissionable quarterly goal is $375,000 with bonuses paid based on sales performance over and above that amount. I will be adding a few surprise sales contests along the way.

Last year, you closed two of the company's ten largest new sales. I know that neither company was easy to sign and I'm really proud of your efforts.

As your manager, I pledge my full support throughout the coming year to help you to achieve your sales goals.

Sincerely,

Mary Smith
President

---

happens when a president combines the hiring of a new rep with the creation of a new compensation plan. While there may be many sound reasons to merge those two events, problems occur if the timing isn't right.

Rushing the plan to completion with the interview process ongoing prevents the president from showing it to their board of directors or peers in their network. Often these valued associates ask questions that help you gain greater clarity or spot potential problems you may not have thought of. The time and trouble it takes to review the plan with others is worth the effort.

Salespeople are notoriously critical of compensation plans, do read the fine print, and will be vocal about their likes and dislikes. If the first criticism of or question about the plan comes from the

Having those in your business network review and critique the plan will increase your confidence level when you discuss it with sales candidates.

job applicant as opposed to a colleague, it can be an unnerving experience. You may react negatively to their questions or objections, even if they have validity.

BE PREPARED TO NEGOTIATE

Experienced sales professionals may look at the compensation plan and try to negotiate with you before they accept a sales position with your company. They might ask for a higher base salary or a higher commission percentage. Certainly they have a right to at least broach the subject with you.

With a compensation plan that's still "warm from the printer" as it's being shown to a candidate, you aren't as sure of yourself. When candidates attempt to negotiate, presidents sometimes acquiesce to the demands too quickly or take a non-negotiable stance that chases the candidate away. You need to be familiar and secure enough with the plan to either consider altering it or let them know that it stands as is.

INCLUDE THE CURRENT STAFF

Adding needed changes to the plan might make you more competitive in your industry or help to attract stronger salespeople to your organization. But a new compensation program will have the greatest impact—at least initially—on your current sales staff. You need the proper amount of lead time to meet with the salespeople and explain the reasoning behind the new pay structure. Give them the time to review the document and be open to discussing any problems or issues they have with it.

Avoid the perception among your current sales staff that this plan was created exclusively for the new sales representative. If you haven't discussed it with them before the new hire joins the company, they may come to this conclusion. They might resent the fact that someone who has not yet made a single sale for the company is the recipient of a new compensation plan. Salespeople can be tough, tough, tough. All major changes or decisions that you make regarding their earning power must take their observations into account.

The new plan may impact your current staff in a positive way. It might *increase* their earning potential. But if you put the plan in place hastily and gave the existing staff no say whatsoever on the details they will react negatively. Objections and questions, even if they were easily fixed or addressed will remain unresolved, bringing the new hire into a negative environment. Avoid this situation.

CREATING A COMPENSATION PLAN

A lot of hard work goes into producing a new compensation plan. It could be that you decided to collaborate with an outside compensation specialist. Perhaps you took on the painstaking task of crafting the new plan yourself. Regardless, the unveiling of a new compensation plan should be an exciting event. Don't cut corners. Take the time to review, finalize, and present it in a way that's balanced and fair for all parties concerned. It's worth the effort.

While this chapter offers guidance on presenting your compensation plan, I don't show you how to design or create one. Many excellent books have been written on that subject, including *The Sales Compensation Handbook* (AMACOM, 1998) by Stockton B. Colt, Jr. and *Compensating the Sales Force* (McGraw-Hill, 2003) by David J. Cichelli. If you're looking to improve or redo the content of your organization's compensation plan, I highly recommend both.

5

Establishing a New Hire Orientation Program

Brent, the president, cannot bear to look out of his office onto the sales floor, so he keeps the door closed. When he does have to leave his office, he invariably sees the new sales representative wandering aimlessly around the office or staring at his computer screen. He finds this very depressing. The new hire has this way of intercepting him, even if he's just going to get more coffee, and anxiously trying to start a conversation.

Often Brent observes him listening intently to the other two sales representatives as they make their sales calls. He wonders why. Some employees have told him that the new hire comes into their cubicles to ask questions. What is he doing in other departments? Brent told him where his territory was and had given him all the product literature to study. He had the opportunity to work with the other sales representative and has a list of the current accounts in his territory. During the interview process he said he was a self-starter who knew how to talk to people. Well, why isn't he self-starting? What is he waiting for?

DURING NEW SALES REPRESENTATIVES' FIRST FEW DAYS ON THE JOB, THEY often work with one or two of the other salespeople before making sales calls in their own territories. Typically, this arrangement benefits new hires. They get to meet the sales staff, watch them work, absorb some product knowledge, and maybe even interact with customers. Once the period of being partnered with another sales representative comes to a close, however, many new hires are left rather abruptly on their own.

New hires want to start selling and be productive as soon as possible. Of course they do. But many feel reluctant to just pick up the phone and start calling customers. They may feel they don't have *quite enough* familiarity with the product, the competition, or the overall market. They want to avoid looking foolish.

Others, once they've called on a few customers, have some questions and don't know where to go to get answers. When they turn to their busy colleagues for assistance, some are more helpful than others. A lot of new sales reps, in their first few weeks, have little direction. Everyone's frustration with "orientation" is understandable.

Because they will be the face or voice of your organization for many of your customers, sales representatives need a longer, more inclusive training period. More than almost any other employee, they need to know a lot about the company they work for. They may only use a small percentage of that knowledge when meeting with a customer. But customers ask different questions about different areas of the company at different times.

>
> **It behooves a salesperson to have solid, broad company and product knowledge; their orientation period is the optimal time to provide it.**

Why does a salesperson need such a comprehensive training period? When you hired a human resource director, they didn't get nearly this amount of attention. What's the difference?

A human resources professional brings portable skills from one employer to another. The HR person's knowledge of discrimination law does not change when he or she switches companies. Employees come to the HR person to discuss maternity leave, not manufacturing capabilities. Managers need to talk about employee disciplinary issues, not the new marketing literature.

Of course HR professionals need time to learn about the new organization and co-workers. Some of the employment laws may be different if they have moved from a large company to a smaller one. Perhaps they will have to handle a difficult personnel situation they've never encountered before. No matter the situation, HR personnel will not be expected to have the company and product knowledge of those in sales.

GETTING BUY-IN

Maybe you recruit top-tier sales professionals to work for your company. Perhaps those same reps are producing at or above your level of expectation for sales revenue. If that's the case, you're hiring the right people, giving them the proper training, and holding them accountable for achieving quota. You might not even need to read this chapter.

But what if you're often dissatisfied with the sales revenue brought in by your new hires? Does your company have a high turnover rate among the sales staff? Are your salespeople perceived as well-trained, confident professionals when they go on that first sales call? Does the sales organization, however large or small, operate like you want it to? If it doesn't, then you need to think about what you as a company are going to do about it.

> **Offering a longer**, more all-encompassing orientation helps presidents put together a well-run sales organization.

If an orientation of this nature is new to your company, you may have to do some "selling" of the idea to the other employees. Before finalizing a schedule, talk to the department heads involved about the:

- Reasons behind improving orientation
- Importance of their participation
- Benefits to the entire company

Show them a tentative schedule. Encourage them to ask questions. Allow them to express doubt. Listen to their opinions. They will undoubtedly make some valuable suggestions.

Money Talks

Some employees may still be skeptical. All that time in orientation? Shouldn't the new sales rep be out selling? Isn't that what he or she was hired to do? Instead of discussing orientation further, *show* the group what turnover and underperformance *costs* your organization. Use a few simple charts to illustrate your point.

Let's say that the sales representatives at your organization have a $1 million annual quota. Historically, if they last a full year, which many do not, new hires achieve about 75% of the quota for the year. With the introduction of a comprehensive orientation program, what if new hires were able to achieve *at a minimum* 90–95% of their quota during that first year? What would that look like?

Figure 5-1. Sales Revenue Gain

	Quota	% of Quota	Sales Revenue
New Hire A	$1,000,000	93%	$930,000
New Hire B	$1,000,000	72%	$720,000
		Difference	$210,000

It looks like $210,000. Not so shabby for a two- to three-week orientation period. The chart above represents sales revenue *gained* when a well-trained sales rep increases production during the first year.

You can show *lost* opportunities to illustrate the same point:

Figure 5-2. Sales Revenue Lost

	3 Month Quota	Production	Sales Revenue
Rep #1	$250,000	50%	$125,000
Rep #2 (not yet hired)	$250,000	0%	0
Total	$500,000		$125,000

In this example, Rep #1 worked Territory A for three months

and then quit. During that time period they achieved about 50% of quota. While your company sourced, interviewed, hired, and trained a new sales representative for the position, the territory remained vacant for three months.

Territory A, worth on average about $500,000 in revenue to your company for the first six months of the year, will only realize $125,000. That's a loss of $375,000 on the year so far.

When your staff considers the loss or gain of a quarter of a million dollars or more, orientation begins to mean something different. They start to view their two- or three-hour involvement with the sales representative as an investment in their company. That amount of money might preserve someone's job or allow another department to add a badly needed staff position. They can contribute to the process. Most will begin to see why the whole idea makes sense.

INCLUDE SALES REPRESENTATIVES

Don't forget to involve the sales staff as you design the orientation schedule. Most have experienced both high- and low-quality new hire orientation and will be able to offer opinions and ideas. Ask them the following about their orientation to your organization:

- What was beneficial to them?
- What was not?
- Overall, did the process help them get acclimated to their new job?
- What could be added to bring the new hire up to speed as quickly as possible?
- What redundancies or omissions exist in the current schedule?
- What has their experience been like at other companies?

Most sales representatives willingly work with new hires to help them learn what they need to know. They've been a new employee themselves and know they may be again at some point. If the compensation plan contains a group bonus component, your current staff will be all the more motivated to help bring the new hire up to speed as soon as possible.

ORIENTATION

While many presidents offer the new hire some product or computer training, most forget to incorporate the rest of the company into orientation. Such departments could include:

- Customer service
- Marketing
- Product development
- Human resources
- Legal
- Reception
- Accounting
- Technical support
- Engineering
- Shipping

Using two departments as an example, I would like to illustrate how a salesperson might benefit from the knowledge gained by spending some time in each one of them.

ENGINEERING

A customer says to a salesperson, "I really wish there were some kind of timing device on your product. I think the first company to add that feature will capture the market." The salesperson replies, "That's an interesting idea. How would you use the timing device? How would it help you? Would you save time or money or both? How do you handle the timing issue now? I'm going to talk to Rhonda, the head of engineering about what you're suggesting."

The salesperson met Rhonda Smith during orientation. He expected her to wear a pocket protector and have almost no personality. Instead she was engaging, taught him a lot about the product, and let him know that she was very interested in direct customer feedback. She encouraged him to tell her what his customers cared about. It took a while for him to get to the point of having in-depth conversations with his customers about new product features, but once he did, he was excited to be able to talk with Rhonda about what they had to say.

Now had the salesperson not spent some time working with Rhonda in engineering, he might have never gotten to know her at all. He might have assumed that she was a "typical engineer" who wanted nothing to do with sales. She might have assumed that he was a "typical salesperson" with no appreciation for the hard work that went into designing new product features. But Rhonda and the salesperson like and respect each other. For as many years as they work together, they will enjoy good communication. The company and the customers will benefit.

ACCOUNTING

In my early years as a sales representative, a customer once handed me a copy of his invoice and said, "Look at how your company screwed up my bill. I expect you to have this fixed." My first thought was, "Oh, that's what one of our invoices looks like!" Too embarrassed to ask questions for fear the customer would realize I was totally unfamiliar with the document, I politely asked him if I could make a copy and take it with me. I apologized for the inconvenience this had caused and promised to call him with an answer as soon as possible.

Back at the office, I found the customer's original order and brought it and the invoice down to accounting. We were able to address the problem and I called the customer back. I was lucky. The customer mistook my staring intently at the invoice as a sign that I was interested in his problem. In reality, the document was completely alien to me and I was staring at it trying to get my bearings. If the customer had caught on to this, it would have made both me and the company look bad.

Salespeople need to be familiar with the billing system. Few of them can avoid angry calls about an error on an invoice. Show them what the invoices look like and how they're generated. Be candid about which sections customers typically have questions on. Ask them if anything on the invoice confuses them or if they have any questions. Going forward, they may be able to talk to customers about the invoices in advance or answer a few questions for them during a sales call—potentially stopping testy calls to customer service. A salesperson with knowledge of the inner workings of a company looks more credible.

YOUR ORIENTATION PROGRAM

Orientation for a sales representative should last at least two or three weeks and take them all around the company. This shocks some business executives. They think, "I can't afford two or three weeks of the salesperson doing nothing but watching the shipping department tape up boxes! Couldn't we complete orientation in a couple of days? I need them out there producing!" Well, you know what? They won't be producing—at least not in a couple of days. The time is better spent teaching them what they need to know. Can you really afford not to?

Besides, selling gets worked into the process. As you review the sample orientation schedule, by Wednesday of week 2 the new hire starts to make prospecting calls. And when they do make those calls, instead of sounding just like a new nervous sales rep, they come across as professional and polished. So after they visit the finance department, have them go make some cold calls. Answer any questions they may have afterward. Send them on to marketing next. You get the picture.

Readers of this book represent all types of industries and offer a variety of products and services. I cannot create a separate orientation schedule for each one to illustrate my recommendations. I use as an example a software company with an inside sales force whose reps occasionally travel to meet with customers and potential clients.

Figure 5-3 to 5-5 show a sample three-week orientation schedule. As you read through it, you may be thinking to yourself, "putting a document like this together looks like a lot of work!" The first time you sit down and develop an orientation schedule like this, it *is* a lot of work. After you have done it once, however,

Figure 5-3. Sample Orientation Schedule Week One

Orientation Schedule
Weeks One through Three
Week One
Monday

Time	Department	Goal
9:00 am–10:00 am	Human Resources	Fill out forms
10:00 am –10:30 am	Company president	Discuss corporate vision and goals
10:30 am–12:00 pm	East Coast sales representative	Monitor sales calls
12:00 pm–1:00 pm	Lunch with EC sales representative	
1:00 pm–1:30 pm	Product Development	Overview of product line
1:30 pm–3:00 pm	Monitor customer service calls	Gain familiarity with customer issues
3:00 pm–3:30 pm	Review sales manual	Focus on introduction and initial objections
3:30 pm–4:30 pm	Meet with sales manager	Review day; answer questions
4:30 pm–5:00 pm	Desk	Study literature on Product A
Tuesday		
9:00 am–10:30 am	Midwest sales representative	Monitor sales calls
10:30 am–12:00 pm	Marketing	Direct mail, lead gen, tradeshows
12:00 pm–1:00 pm	Lunch w/Midwest sales rep	
1:00 pm–4:00 pm	IT	Get passwords set up; learn company software
4:00 pm–4:30 pm	Review material for Product B	Think of 3 questions for each product
4:30 pm–5:00 pm	Meet with sales manager	Review day; discuss product questions
Wednesday		
9:00 am–10:00 am	Conference Room A	Sales staff meeting
10:00 am–11:00 am	West Coast sales representative	Observe Webex demonstration on Product A
11:00 am–12:00 pm	Accounting	Sales order entry, invoicing, and receivables
12:00 pm–1:00 pm	Lunch w/ WC sales representative	
1:00 pm–5:00 pm	EC sales representative	Meet local area customers/prospects
Thursday		
8:00 am–4:00 pm	The Computer Institute	Offsite all day, sales software training
Friday		
8:00 am–4:00 pm	The Computer Institute	Offsite all day, sales software training

Weekend assignment: Review sales manual chapters on introduction and qualifying questions. Be prepared for role play.

Figure 5-4 Orientation Schedule Week Two

Week Two Monday		
Time	**Department**	**Goal**
9:00 am–10:00 am	East Coast rep	Role play prospecting calls, intro/qualifying questions
10:00 am –11:30 am	Shipping	Observe how software is packaged/shipped
11:30 am–12:30 pm	Midwest rep	Watch Webex on Product A
12:30 pm–1:30 pm	Lunch	
1:30 pm–2:30 pm	Desk	Practice Webex on Product A
2:30 pm–4:00 pm	Sales manager/West Coast rep	Give a Webex Demo of Product A
4:00 pm–4:30 pm	Study sales manual	Review standard objections/needs assessment questions
4:30 pm–5:00 pm	Meet with sales manager	Role play standard objections/needs assessment questions
Tuesday		
9:00 am–10:00 am	Reception	Observe incoming calls
10:00 am–11:00 am	Marketing	Discuss positioning of product line
11:00 am–11:30 am	Desk	Take test on Product A
11:30 am–12:30 pm	Desk	Practice Webex on Product A
12:30 pm–1:30 pm	Lunch	
1:30 pm–3:00 pm	Sales Manager	Give a Webex demo of Product A
3:00 pm–4:00 pm	Technical Support	Observe customer calls
4:00 pm–5:00 pm	Midwest sales rep	Role play prospecting calls
7:00 pm–9:00 pm	Sales College	Begin sales training course
Wednesday		
9:00 am–10:00 am	Conference Room A	Sales staff meeting
10:00 am–10:30 am	Sales Manager	Discuss results of Product A Quiz/Webexes
10:30 am–12:00 pm	Desk	Prospect to "dead" accounts list
12:00 pm–1:00 pm	Lunch	
1:00 pm–2:00 pm	East Coast rep	Observe Webex Demo for Product B
2:00 pm–3:00 pm	Desk	Practice Webex Demo for Product B
3:00 pm–4:30 pm	Desk	Prospect to "dead" accounts list
4:30 pm–5:00 pm	Sales Manager	Discuss major accounts report

Figure 5-4 Orientation Schedule Week Two (continued)

Week Two Thursday		
Time	**Department**	**Goal**
9:00 am–10:00 am	Marketing	Review brochures, collateral material
10:00 am –11:00 am	Desk	Study Product B
11:00 am–11:30 am	Product Development	Discuss Product B
11:30 pm–12:00 pm	Product Development	Take test for Product B
12:00 pm–1:00 pm	Lunch	
1:00 pm–4:30 pm	Technical Representative	Accompany local area tech rep on customer calls
4:30 pm–5:00 pm	Sales Manager	Review Product B test results
Friday		
9:00 am–10:00 am	Desk	Prospect
10:00 am–11:00 am	West Coast rep	Discuss positioning of product line
11:00 am–12:00 pm	Engineering	CTO talks about technical vision for company
12:00 pm–1:00 pm	Lunch	
1:00 pm–2:00pm	Sales Manager	Mock sale from cold call to demo
2:00 pm–4:00 pm	Desk	Generate proposal
4:00 pm–5:00 pm	Sales Manager	Present proposal to sales manager; ask for sale
Weekend Assignment: Read and study major accounts report.		

Figure 5-5. Orientation Schedule Week 3

Week Three Monday		
Time	**Department**	**Goal**
9:00 am–10:00 am	Desk	Practice Webex for Product B
10:00 am–11:00 am	Sales Manager	Give Webex of Product B
11:00 am–12:30 pm	Desk	Prospect "dead account" list
12:30 pm–1:30 pm	Lunch	
1:30 pm–3:00 pm	Desk	Study major account report
3:00 pm–4:00 pm	Desk	Review sales manual, Objections/ Interview Questions
4:00 pm–5:00 pm	Midwest rep	Role play common objections/ interview questions

Figure 5-5. Orientation Schedule Week 3 (continued)

**Week Three
Tuesday**

Time	Department	Goal
9:00 am–10:00 am	Desk	Role play: conduct an interview with prospect from "dead acct." list
10:30 am–11:00 am	Sales Manager	Critique of interview
11:00 am–12:30 pm	Desk	Prospect "dead account" list
12:30 pm–1:30 pm	Lunch	
1:30 pm–3:00 pm	Desk	Continue to prospect
3:00 pm–4:00 pm	Desk	Review contracts/proposals/section of binder
4:00 pm–5:00 pm	Midwest rep	Generate proposal for new prospect
7:00 pm–9:00 pm	Sales College	Sales training course
Wednesday		
9:00 am–10:00 am	Conference Room A	Sales staff meeting
10:30 am–11:30 am	Desk	Give Webinar to interested prospect from "dead" accounts list
11:00 am–12:30 pm	Sales Manager	Critique interview
12:30 pm–1:30 pm	Lunch	
1:30 pm–2:30 pm	East Coast rep	Monitor customer interview
3:00 pm–4:00 pm	Desk	Review Contract /Proposals section of manual
4:00 pm–5:00 pm	Midwest rep	Generate proposal for new prospect
Thursday		
9:00 am–10:00 am	Sales Manager	Review sales reporting system
10:00 am–11:00 am	Desk	Create sample pipeline/opportunity and sales forecast reports
11:00 am–12:30 pm	Desk	Prospecting calls
12:30 pm–1:30 pm	Lunch	
1:30 pm–3:30 pm	Desk	Prospecting calls
3:30 pm–4:30 pm	Desk	Review proposal sent to new prospect
4:30 pm–5:00 pm	Sales Manager	Be prepared to discuss each major acct

Figure 5-5. Orientation Schedule Week 3 (continued)

Week Three Friday		
Time	**Department**	**Goal**
9:00 am–10:00 am	Desk	Prospect
10:00 am–11:00 am	Desk	Create schedule for next week
11:00 am–12:00 pm	West Coast rep	Webex of Products A and B
12:00 pm–1:00 pm	Lunch	
1:00 pm–2:00 pm	Sales Manager	Discuss schedule
3:00 pm–4:00 pm	IT	Review use of software
4:00 pm–5:00 pm	Desk	Prospect

the basic template doesn't change. Yes, you'll have to make allowances for those who might be traveling or on vacation. Once you've had a sales representative or two go through the orientation, you may find that there needs to be more emphasis on some things and less on others. You can work with the template, though, for many years.

IMPORTANCE OF GOALS

In my sample schedule, the word *Goal* heads the third column. Many times I've observed new sales representatives as they work with someone in a different department. Often they are staring into space or looking bored. Unfortunately, most have no idea why they're there or what they're supposed to be learning.

Give them a clipboard, pen, and worksheet for every department they visit and watch the energy change. If they are sitting alongside the receptionist, ask them to record how many departments received calls. Repeat the experience with customer service: How many calls did the customer service rep handle? What was the average length of the call? What types of questions did the customers most frequently ask? Where does customer serv-

> **New salespeople need to have an end result in mind when they work with another individual in the company.**

ice go for the answers?

New hires don't need to spend all day in certain departments. They will learn a lot during a solid hour with the receptionist or customer service representative. As a sales manager, when I would ask sales representatives how things went in reception, they always made comments such as "That's a hard job. They put up with a lot. I never knew."

No matter which department they visit, they will come away with a respect for that individual's job. Both parties will enjoy a slightly more personalized relationship from having spent some time together.

Lunch

Will their new boss take them out to lunch on the first day or will they be on their own? Should they brown bag it? Will they even get a lunch break on that first day? If they do bring a lunch, can they eat at their desk? Does the a company lunch room? Will they be sitting there all by themselves or do the employees eat together? The midday meal can be awkward for new hires.

When I was a sales manager, I would ask one or two of the sales representatives if they would be willing to go out to lunch with the new hire on the first day. I would ask another sales representative to do so the next day. I never had anyone turn me down. People understand how awkward it can be and are typically happy to help out.

Lunch also gives the new hire an opportunity to meet new colleagues in a low-key situation. After the first week, I found that new hires had figured out what the lunchtime protocol was (spoken or unspoken) and they were fine on their own. Many thanked me for organizing their first few lunches. I was glad to make the extra effort for them.

Be Flexible

After working hard to create the orientation schedule, get ready for some unplanned glitches. The entire engineering group might have to work around the clock to meet a new product deadline and cannot even think about making time for your new hire. Another employee could have an unforeseen emergency. While making the first few prospecting calls, new sales representatives might stumble onto an honest-to-goodness potential customer who wants to meet with them in the next few days. In other words, things happen that are out of your control.

Be empathetic when someone has an unforeseen conflict. Reschedule whenever possible. But keep in mind that orientation is a process that should be *completed*. Make sure that the new hire circles back and works with engineering once they finish the product launch. Provide the proper support when they go on that first appointment to meet a new prospect. They might not be really "ready" to sell yet. The whole exercise will really boost their self-confidence. Reschedule with the employee who needed to see to his or her personal emergency. Your flexibility will be remembered and appreciated.

DETRACTORS

Despite all of your best efforts to take everyone's thoughts into account, some employees might not rise to the occasion during orientation. Certain staff members may look down on or buy into common stereotypes about salespeople. They may say something like "Salespeople make a lot of money just running around all day talking to people. I actually work." Though they may find orientation to be a good idea theoretically, other employees may resent having to take the time out of their day to participate.

Speak directly with the individuals involved. Assume the positive. Depending on the scope of their position with your company, they may not interact with people a lot. Certain employees may feel awkward talking to a sales rep about what they do. Help these people out. Make suggestions about what they might discuss with the new rep. Reiterate the importance of their contribution.

Most importantly, look to your new hires for clues. When I would ask them about a visit to a certain department during orien-

Don't send the new hires to meet with a caustic or negative employee. Make arrangements for them to learn that particular information some other way.

tation, I could usually tell whether it had been productive or not. If they seemed enthusiastic and provided me with details about what he or she had learned, I knew it had gone well.

If they gave me a tight smile or spoke in vague generalities I felt pretty certain it had been a waste of everyone's time. If any employee makes new hire orientation a difficult or unpleasant experience, I would certainly remember that when it comes time for their annual performance review.

SMALL COMPANIES

In reading the orientation schedule you may have thought to yourself, "That's great but there are only five of us in our company." Or "We have never nor will we ever have a receptionist." Or "We don't have any other sales representatives for the new hire to work with. She's the first one we've hired."

I completely understand, but accept no excuses. If there are only five employees, I'm willing to bet that a lot of company knowledge exists among the five of you. Discuss what the new hire needs to know to effectively represent your product or service and divide the responsibilities up accordingly.

Though beneficial, not being able to work with another sales representative doesn't spell doom for the new hire. Think out of the box. Pay close attention to my thoughts on sales training in Chapter 10. That will help with the sales component of orientation.

The sales representative knowingly accepted a job with a very small company. This rep has signed up for and understands some of the challenges. Devise an orientation that works for your size business. The new rep will recognize and appreciate the thought and effort that you put into it.

THE MISTAKE-FREE ORIENTATION

Most importantly, try and remember that no perfect orientation schedule exists. Don't get dragged down by minutiae. You are offering new salespeople a broad-based education on your organization and exposure to the knowledge necessary to sell your products or services.

No matter how thorough the orientation, they will still make a mistake or two on a sales call out of inexperience and nervousness. They will forget the answer to a customer's question. Overall, though, they will carry themselves as a more confident and informed professional salesperson.

Sit down and think through the process. Enlist the help of others. Schedule departments one by one and it will fall together.

Part Two

Setting Expectations for the New Hire

6

Creating a
Sales Toolkit

Anthony, the new sales representative, scribbles furiously on his yellow legal pad. As his colleague Carlene introduces herself to a prospect, he tries to write down everything she says. Her introduction sounds so friendly, natural, and fluid that Anthony would like to say the same thing when he calls his prospects. He worries about Carlene's reaction, though, if she were to overhear him using her opening words line-for-line.

In the cubicle to Anthony's left, Don, one of the other salespeople, begins a product demonstration. Anthony admires Don's "all the time in the world" attitude as he skillfully and patiently directs the prospect through the demonstration. Don's calm demeanor belies the fact that he has the highest demo-to-closed-sale ratio on the sales staff. Anthony would really like his assistance in improving his own closing skills, but feels reluctant to approach him. Don is so busy and successful.

Anthony notices Carlene leaving her cubicle. With Don conducting a demo and Carlene away from her desk, this might be the perfect time to make a few calls using her introduction. Neither one of them will be the wiser.

SUCH ARE THE CHOPPY WATERS THAT MANY SALESPEOPLE NAVIGATE WHEN they first join new companies. It need not be this difficult. A better way exists.

Let's look at a parallel situation. Can you imagine, even for a moment, an NFL coach holding the team playbook back from a rookie player? Can you envision that coach saying to the freshly signed rookie, "Didn't you play football in high school *and* in college? Why do you need a playbook? You know how to play the game. Just go out there and play football!"

Common sense tells you that it simply wouldn't happen, right? The playbook helps the rookie understand the team's *specific* system. It spells out the strategies and tactics the team will use to address as many situations as the coach thinks the team will encounter.

But daily, in thousands of sales offices across the country, intelligent, well-meaning business executives send new sales reps out to sell without a playbook. Instead of passing plays and defensive schemes, the sales playbook (also referred to as a toolkit or manual) contains material that helps sales reps articulate the value of their company's *specific* products or services. It assists them in every step of the sales process.

Companies failing to provide a toolkit for new hires unknowingly increase the amount of time it **takes these reps to become a productive member of the sales staff.**

Though critically important to a new salesperson's success in the early going, and relatively easy to produce, few companies invest the time and resources to create a sales toolkit. Avoid this common sales management pitfall by creating one that contains the following:

- Introductions/voicemail scripts
- Templates for e-mail correspondence
- Qualifying questions
- Interview questions
- Common customer objections
- Objection responses
- Sample closes

Assembling a sales toolkit does require some work and many presidents worry that the entire job will fall to them. Luckily though, a toolkit involves coordinating the efforts of staff members

At this point, you might wonder where you will find the time for all this sales stuff. So far I've asked you to create a customized welcome letter, write a compensation plan, and plot out a three-week, hour-by-hour schedule for your new sales hire. You also know that before the end of this book, I'll very likely come up with more things for you to do. (You're right!) But trust me—stick with it. This will all pay off.

connected to sales as opposed to the president doing everything. Much of the information needed to fill the sales manual is already known by the employees, just not written down.

Many people think of a sales toolkit as exclusive to large companies with sizable marketing departments and big budgets. They picture customized three-ring binders with fancy graphics and integrated e-learning software, or an internal company website that requires constant care and feeding. While many large companies can and do produce slick-looking toolkits, the aesthetics matter less than the quality and timeliness of the information inside

You may wonder why a sales toolkit is really a necessity for your company. If you hired someone who can sell, shouldn't they already know this stuff? Shouldn't they come prepared knowing how to introduce themselves to a prospective client or address an objection? Once they have all that figured out, wouldn't the toolkit be useless?

Yes, new hires possess some pre-existing skills and will gradually figure out what they need to know. Through trial and error, they will create an introduction; learn the most common objections, and determine the approach to closing that makes the most sense. Here's the bad news: the commodity they will use to gain all of this knowledge is time—your time!

You and your better sales reps already know what the new hires need to know. Without the toolkit, you're forcing them to reinvent the wheel. It will take new hires months to put all the pieces into a cohesive sales process. During this period their productivity suffers and they lose sales by making avoidable mistakes.

The news gets worse, I'm afraid. Without a toolkit, when new hires complete their "self-training" you might not approve of the way they have chosen to, for example, introduce themselves, or close sales. If no standard introduction or closing methodology exists within your organization, it will be difficult for you to then get them to do things differently. They may resent the criticism. Most probably, they will continue to introduce themselves or close the sale in a way that is comfortable for them but not necessarily for you.

Imagine your NFL team again. If that rookie didn't receive and memorize the playbook, what would happen when he went onto the field? I'll tell you: The play would start and he wouldn't know where to run, whom to block, or whom to cover. Both the rookie and the team would suffer from his lack of preparation. Don't set your new salesperson up for failure; produce and deliver a quality sales playbook.

An executive once said to me, "One of my former sales reps had the best introduction. Every time I heard her use it, I would think 'that's really good.' I only wish I'd gotten her to write it down." By not capturing and recording the best sales practices of your company, you're missing an opportunity to establish a sales methodology. You're also letting your intellectual capital walk out the door when a sales rep resigns.

HISTORY

While doing research for this book, I read a fascinating book by Penrose Scull entitled *From Peddlers to Merchant Princes: A History of Selling in America* (Follet Publishing Company, 1967). He tells the following story about sales training:

> In 1884 The National Cash Register Company employed thirteen people and produced four or five cash registers per week. By 1887, this same company employed thirty salesmen and sold nearly 12,000 cash registers during that three-year period.
>
> Salesman Joseph H. Crane had the best record for overcoming the sales resistance and writing the most orders. Crane

believed his success was due largely to a carefully prepared sales talk he had written. In the past, he felt that he had missed out on many a sale due to what he saw as his "hit or miss" presentation. So he sat down and wrote out his sales presentation word for word, making sure to cover all of the salient points. He memorized it and never deviated from it when selling a prospect. Crane wrote what is believed to be the first "canned" sales presentation.

John H. Patterson, the owner of The National Cash Register Company, listened to Crane's presentation, realized it was good, and had it printed into pamphlet form with the title "The N.C.R. Primer" and the subtitle "How I Sell a Cash Register." The pamphlet was circulated to all National salesmen and agents, who were told to learn the presentation word for word. So far as can be determined, NCR was the first company to prepare for its salesmen such a set sales talk.

GETTING STARTED

To start the project, consider each bulleted topic that I listed on page 66. Ask yourself which of your salespeople does the most effective job in each category. Who has the most compelling introduction, asks the best qualifying questions, addresses objections effectively, or possesses the strongest closing techniques?

As you begin to answer these questions, approach the various reps and ask them to write down their introduction or their qualifying questions, for example, and e-mail them to you. During staff meetings, share what they sent with the rest of the sales staff. Ask for their input. Undoubtedly, the group will have many interesting ideas to add.

If no one sales representative excels at a particular topic, brainstorm with all of the sales reps during a staff meeting and record the best suggestions. Proceed section by section in this manner.

Gathering your sales staff together to discuss how they introduce themselves or address an objection results in the group sharing best practices. They will pick up tips from each other and learn how their peers handle difficult sales situations. Toolkits review

Current staff members benefit from helping to put together a sales toolkit.

sales basics and best practices. Every salesperson needs that type of information from time to time. Before making a sales call, good sales reps will often consult some type of sales manual to refresh their memory on a certain sales topic or technique. Why not be the person that shapes and controls that "Sales 101" content for your organization?

In my first position as a sales manager in the corporate world, I managed an experienced and well-paid sales staff. Though cordial to each other, most were focused, kept to themselves, and participated in very little shop talk. I told my immediate boss (the director of sales) and his boss (the vice president of sales) that I wanted to start a weekly discussion group. My general thought was that the salespeople should come to the meeting prepared to discuss a customer objection or an issue they were struggling with. This would allow them to discuss the situation with their peers.

Both my boss and the vice president were skeptical, citing the experience level of the group. My managers also felt that their status as top performers would be a deterrent to any meaningful conversation or exchange of ideas. I stood my ground and insisted that we give it a try.

As the group filed in for the first meeting, I was a bundle of nerves, fearing it would be a total disaster. The first salesperson talked about a dilemma he was having with a customer. To my relief, another rep jumped right in with, "You know, I tried this when I was having that same problem and it worked!" The most senior and top salesperson at the company said, "You're kidding. Did you really say that? Let me write that down…"

My boss and the vice president, who attended the meeting despite their skepticism, started adding comments, and the meeting took off from there. Everyone participated, and the more senior members of the group took most of the notes.

Later, my bosses admitted surprise at the meeting's success. They had feared that the egos in the room would stymie any meaningful conversation or that the top producers would refuse to admit that they were struggling with anything. They encouraged me to proceed with my idea of holding the meetings on a weekly basis. In addition, we began a dialog about future sales training for this group.

Typically, salespeople will share information if one of their peers comes to them for help. They aren't proactive when it comes to offering guidance and tips to the new hire, though. Some assume that's someone else's job. Others feel awkward about it. When a meeting gets arranged for them and they feel supported in a non-critical environment, the helpful information usually flows.

For many of my clients, assembling the sales toolkit begins a discovery process. Usually, they are amazed by all of the information that already exists among their employees. Meaningful sales discussions between staff members continue long after the handbook is completed.

One Rep Only

Many readers may only have one sales rep in their company and wonder if a sales manual for a single rep makes sense. It makes perfect sense. Without fellow sales colleagues to bounce ideas off of and learn from, this salesperson really needs the support and information a toolkit offers.

Sit down with these solo sales reps and find out how they introduce themselves. Discover what types of questions they ask potential clients. During this process you will undoubtedly uncover parts of the sales cycle in which these representatives excel and parts where they could use some coaching. Add some of your considerable expertise or hire some outside help to fill in gaps. Identify areas where the toolkit could benefit from the contributions of other staff members. Ask for their help. The salespeople will benefit immeasurably.

THE INTRODUCTION

Poor introductions are painful to listen to. Unfortunately, new salespeople often struggle to come up with a strong, compelling introduction. As a consequence, they face a lot of unnecessary rejection during their first attempts at making prospecting calls.

During the introduction, salespeople have to tell a prospect:

- Who they are
- Whom they work for
- What the company does
- How their company's product or service might benefit the prospect

A compelling introduction needs to capture prospects' interest and keep them on the phone long enough to answer a few questions. The benefits of the product or service must be persuasive enough for the prospect to agree to speak with the sales representative further. Compressing all the above information into a succinct statement challenges even experienced sales representatives.

Top-performing salespeople use more than one introduction to fit different types of prospecting calls. They also practice those introductions until they sound conversational. A compelling introduction combines business acumen and acting. A salesperson who has one has a better chance of continuing the discussion with a decision-maker. Here's what a strong introduction sounds like:

Mr. Prospect, my name is Jane Salesperson and I'm with Acme Repair, the top commercial washer and dryer repair company in our metro area. We help reduce tenant complaints about broken washers and dryers by adhering to a regular maintenance schedule and we arrive at your location within two hours, guaranteed. Is washer and dryer maintenance something you'd like to hear a little bit more about?

With some editing, most introductions can serve as a strong voicemail:

Mr. Prospect, my name is Jane Salesperson and I'm with Acme Repair, the top commercial washer and dryer repair company in our metro area. We help reduce tenant complaints about broken washers and dryers by adhering to a regular maintenance schedule and we repair broken machines within two hours, guaranteed. If washer and dryer maintenance is something you'd like to hear a little bit more about, I'd welcome the opportunity to speak with you about it. My number is xxx-xxx-xxxx. If I don't hear back from you, I will call you tomorrow between 4:00 pm and 5:00 pm. Again, this is Jane Salesperson with Acme Repair. I look forward to speaking with you Mr. Prospect.

Work with your sales staff, individually and collectively, writing several high-impact introductions and voicemail messages to add to the sales toolkit. Everyone will benefit from the exercise, not just your new hire.

> **Art Sobczak of Business By Phone, Inc. provides excellent advice on creating strong introductions. Sign up for his newsletter at www.businessby-phone.com.**

CORRESPONDENCE TEMPLATES

Ask those who manage salespeople if a letter or an e-mail sent out by a new hire has ever caused embarrassment. The pained look on their face will serve as confirmation. Gaffes include: poor grammar, too much information, inappropriate content, misspelled words, incorrect pricing, and unauthorized guarantees. Many people in the workplace (salespeople and non-sales types, alike) do not possess solid business writing skills. Hence the need for, and wisdom of, creating templates for business correspondence.

New salespeople are particularly prone to difficulties when it comes to written correspondence. Lack of familiarity with all aspects of their new company results in letters and e-mails that look amateurish and create a poor image. For this reason, I often advise managers to require that all new sales representatives send out only approved "templated" correspondence.

At some point, salespeople may want to add some of their own content. Consider the new salesperson's creative ideas and input but reserve the right to review any and all written material being sent to customers and prospects.

A small library of correspondence templates should include:

- Introductory letter
- Thank you letter
- Follow-up letter

An *introductory letter* serves the same purpose as the telephone introduction but in written form. The letter should say just enough but not too much. Rather than attempting to interest a potential client in their product or service, many new or inexperienced sales representatives include too much or irrelevant information. This causes recipients to lose interest rather than be intrigued.

Thank you letters serve multiple purposes. Salespeople might want to express appreciation to a prospect for taking the time to meet with them, thank a customer for introducing them to a colleague, or acknowledge a customer for purchasing a product or service from their company. Salespeople may have lost a sale but would like to maintain a cordial relationship with a prospect. They may want to convey gratitude to a long-time, loyal customer. Thank you notes require care to write and should never be overused. A manager needs to review any sent out to ensure they have the proper tone.

The *follow-up letter* reviews what was discussed during a phone conversation or face-to-face meeting and confirms the next steps to be taken for both the prospect and the salesperson. A follow up letter acts as a bridge as the sale progresses from one part of the sales cycle to the next. Be aware that a new hire with weak closing skills might try to use a letter like this to close a sale.

I recommend an inventory of a few different types of follow up letters for each stage of your sales cycle such as:

- Introduction follow-up
- Presentation follow-up
- Demonstration follow-up
- Proposal follow-up

Dear Joe,

Thank you for speaking with me last week regarding Acme Repair's commercial washer and dryer services. Based on our conversation, I understand your key requirements to be:

• Improved coin slots
• Same day service
• Guarantee on all repair work

At your request, I have sent a sample of the coin slot we have had great success with. Please find attached a copy of our repair warranty and two-hour response time guarantee.

I look forward to continuing our discussion on August 8 at 8:30 am.

Have a nice weekend.

Jane Salesperson

Here is an example of an introduction follow-up e-mail:

Jane Salesperson recognizes that the decision-maker took time out of his day to discuss her company's services. She demonstrates that she understands which of her company's products might best suit his needs, acknowledges his concerns, and confirms that she sent relevant samples and documents. Before ending the conversation, Jane and the customer agreed on a specific date and time for another conversation, which she makes note of. These are trademark components of a strong follow-up letter.

Written correspondence, thanks to technology, permeates our lives like never before. Gone are the days when a letter gets filed away and/or thrown out. E-mail and texting have made almost all written communication permanent. Salespeople need to be careful about anything they send to customers, and managers need to be vigilant about overseeing correspondence sent.

QUALIFYING QUESTIONS

These questions baffle even seasoned sales reps. What defines a qualifying question? At what point in the sale should they be used? How are they different from other questions? The confusion makes creating a list of effective qualifying questions tricky business. If not asked in the right way and at the proper time, these questions can alienate a potential client.

Used early in the sales process, qualifying questions help a salesperson determine if prospects could *potentially* use the company's product or service—not *will they* but *could they*. In asking qualifying questions, a sales rep might discover that a prospect really has no need for what the company offers. This can be disheartening, especially for new hires who are eager to fill their pipeline and don't want to disqualify any company.

Here are some examples of qualifying questions:

- How is maintenance handled in your apartment building?
- Do you have washers and dryers in your building?
- What happens when a washer or dryer breaks down?
- What sort of agreement do you have with that company?

Together with your sales staff, come up with a list of questions that help sales representatives gather the preliminary information they need. With most questions, the prospect should be able to give more than a one-word answer.

Encourage new hires to ask these high-value questions. Assure them that it's perfectly OK to discover that a company cannot use your product or service—and the earlier in the sales process the better. Then monitor the new sales representatives' prospecting calls to ensure that they are asking these questions and paying close attention to the answers.

INTERVIEW QUESTIONS

Once a prospect has been qualified as having genuine interest in and a need for a product or service, the salesperson makes an appointment for an in-depth conversation, either in person or over the phone. These sales interview sessions have the potential for disaster. Unsure of exactly which questions to ask and how much information they should come away with, new hires either ramble on and waste the prospect's time or ask too few questions.

When the meeting ends they might not have the proper information needed to move the sale forward. Many eager new hires tend to overestimate the prospect's level of interest and end up making too many draining "just checking in" calls. Worse yet, they add disinterested prospects into the pipeline or the sales forecast, where they may languish for weeks or months.

Avoiding this requires assembling a list of high-impact, high-value questions for your sales force to ask. It helps if you organize the questions by category and include potential follow-up questions. Figure 6-1 on the next page shows an example of how this works.

New hires will have to work at making these questions sound conversational. By providing them with interview questions, you increase the chances that they will complete their first meetings with a greater understanding of each prospect's needs and level of interest.

CUSTOMER OBJECTIONS AND RESPONSES

Salespeople who have been in the profession for any length of time know that there are three or four common objections that prospects typically bring up during sales calls. Yes, once in a while salespeople will encounter an objection that they've never heard before. Or a company might have a unique situation customers will ask about (a problem with their new software, for example). Most objections repeat themselves and therefore should not catch a salesperson off-guard.

New sales hires expect to hear customer objections. They are, after all, part of every sales process. Being new to your organization, they don't know the *specifics* of the objections their prospect might bring up about your product or service and aren't practiced at addressing them.

> **For great information on the hows and whys of objections,** read Linda Richardson's classic Stop Telling Start Selling (McGraw-Hill, 1998).

An example of an objection and response common to your organization is shown in Figure 6-2 on page 79.

Together with your sales reps, put together a list of the most common objections and get input from them on how they address these objections.

Figure 6-1. Interview Questions

Product/Service Questions	Follow-ups
Can you tell me about your current repair service?	What do you like about doing business with them?
Have there been any difficulties in dealing with that particular company?	How have they resolved those issues?
How would a two-hour response time like ours benefit you?	In what ways would that benefit impact the renters?
What's been the response on the part of the tenants to the jammed coin slots?	Whom do they complain to?

Organizational Questions	Follow-ups
What prompted you to consider a change in repair companies?	How do others at your management company feel about a potential change?
Where does this rank on your priority list?	In what ways would that benefit impact the renters?
How will you involve employees in this decision-making process?	Why those particular employees?
If you did switch over to us, what type of paperwork or process would be involved?	Who would be in charge of that?

Budget Questions	Follow-ups
How does the budgeting process work at your company?	How would an annual maintenance contract figure into your budget?
What is your level of involvement in the budgeting process?	Has it always been that way?
Do you have any other major capital expenditures planned for the year?	How are they prioritized?

CLOSING

Closing the deal is both the simplest and the most psychologically complex skill in the entire sales cycle. Managers and presidents alike say to me, "I need to hire a closer." Many complain about

Figure 6-2. Responses to Objections

Objection	Response
Your price is higher than the other repair company's.	Negotiating the best price is the main concern at most companies. We try and get the best deal at our company, too.
	Can I ask you which services of ours were higher?
	Does that include regular maintenance and the guaranteed two hour arrival time?
	How much revenue do you lose if the dryers aren't working for a few days?
	I understand that you like the prices your current vendor offers. At first glance, our services do appear to cost more. If I can demonstrate an overall savings, will you accept a quote from us?

salespeople who possess excellent prospecting or qualifying skills but often need management assistance to get a sale closed. Having to close deals for a salesperson wears down most sales managers and creates a sense of dependency for the sales representative.

Taking the time to put a toolkit together makes the job of closing a sale easier. If sales representatives follow time-tested guidelines throughout the sales cycle, they will have a much better understanding of which prospects are most likely to buy. No matter their level of certainty about the prospect's level of interest, though, they must come right out and ask for the business in the end.

Once again, start with your current staff before you begin assembling the closing section of the toolkit. Find out who has the highest closing rate. How does the sales rep know when the prospect is ready to buy? Find out how this person approaches the close. Why does that approach work? Who has trouble closing? What do they say that might be different from what the strong closer says? Meet with your sales team and get their general thoughts on the closing process. Ask them to share their closing statements with you.

Despite how critical a skill it is, many salespeople—new hires and tenured alike—receive little or no training geared specifically to closing sales.

Closing a sale involves a salesperson's ability to:

- Ask trial close questions
- Recognize buying signals
- Formally ask for business

TRIAL CLOSE

Using a trial close allows a salesperson to determine the prospect's true interest level with regard to purchasing the company's product or service. Being asked a trial question is an uncomfortable experience for some prospects—especially if they aren't really interested in buying. It puts them on the spot. After being asked a trial close question, many will come right out and admit that they will very likely be purchasing from another vendor. Here are some examples of trial close questions:

- Considering what we've discussed during our meetings, what are your thoughts on Acme Repair?
- You're considering my company and the company you've been using for many years. How do we compare?
- If you had to make a decision today, which company do you think you would choose?

Sometimes, new or inexperienced reps, wanting to avoid chasing any potential customer away, will refrain from asking these critical questions. Create the toolkit and then encourage them to use trial close questions. Remind them that knowing how and when to use a trial close will decrease the amount of time they waste on prospects who will never commit to buying.

BUYING SIGNALS

Buying signals are verbal and non-verbal cues that prospects are ready to purchase the salesperson's product or service. Prospects may lean forward and speak more rapidly or may tip back in the chair and speak more slowly. Some people fidget nervously. The reaction depends on the individual. All prospects that are ready to buy have one thing in common: they are picturing actually using your product or service. They can envision owning it. As a result, they ask "action" questions such as:

- How would we go about …?
- What's the soonest you could …?
- If the accounting department was willing to…?
- What would the cost of _____ be?
- Would a September delivery be realistic?

Though new hires have undoubtedly heard action questions before, interested prospects will ask questions *specific* to your product or service. New hires might not recognize as buying signals in the beginning. Meet with your salespeople and make a list of them. Once new hires familiarize themselves with those questions, they will be able to more quickly ascertain when a prospect is ready to buy.

FORMALLY ASK FOR THE BUSINESS

After sales representatives have made one or more presentations to a prospect, rescheduled meetings, addressed endless objections, responded to numerous requests for information, and then generated a proposal, they want the customer to tell them that they are ready to do business. Seems only fair, after all the work they put in, right? Too bad it doesn't work that way.

No matter how great a match the product or service might be for the prospect's business or how attractive the price point, most of the time the sales representative has to ask for the business directly. Many reps dread asking because they might hear the word "no." A rejection, after all that work, would really hurt.

Though they want to avoid rejection, new hires have other concerns, as well. They might not have built up a large pipeline of prospects yet. Their sales forecast may not be as full as they would like. Pipelines and forecasts with a lot of prospects listed show how hard they have been working and the amount of sales revenue they could potentially bring in. By not asking for the sale, they can avoid removing a prospect from their pipeline or forecast.

Presidents need to tell the new hire that not getting a final answer from a client is detrimental to the company and to their careers. Remind new hires that by asking trial close questions and observing potential buying signals, the chances are strong that the prospect will say yes.

As with all the other issues addressed in the training binder, the new salesperson has undoubtedly closed a sale or two before. You should ask what words were used to close those sales. If you like what you hear, great. If not, tell the new salesperson to use the formal closes that your sales staff provided you with.

A strong close might come in the following form:

Mr. Apartment Building Owner, you've had a persistent problem with jammed coin slots in your Oak Street building. Kwik Fix makes the repair, only to have them jam again. Those dryers are sometimes out of service for two days. With the brand of coin slots we use, our regular maintenance visits and our two hour response time, Acme Repair can decrease both the down-time on the machines and customer complaints. Should we move forward with a maintenance agreement?

Arming them with suggested closes will result in fewer blown sales, and a shorter sales cycle. Including this information in the toolkit will minimize the opportunities for a rep to procrastinate in closing the sale. The new hire will recognize buying signals and then confidently ask for the prospect's business

Overall Benefit

By creating a sales toolkit, you bring together in one document the specific sales skills needed for success at your company. It is a win-win situation for the new hire, the current staff, and future additions to the sales staff.

The sales skills section does not complete the toolkit, however. Well-trained and prepared sales professionals need to be knowledgeable about the history of their new company, all major competitors, and the specifics of the product or service they will be selling. In the following chapter, I explain the creation of this next section of the sales toolkit in detail.

7

Assembling Collateral Material

"I'm not sure. I'll ask our sales engineer and call you back with an answer," Joelle said sheepishly to her prospect. It was the fourth technical question she had been unable to answer so far. "Would you please ask the sales engineer to call me directly?" asked the prospect in an unfriendly tone. Feeling that the sale might be lost no matter how she handled the request, she just said "Sure, I'd be happy to." After a few uncomfortable pleasantries, she packed up her laptop and left the prospect's office.

Joelle knew her technical and competitive knowledge was weak. To improve the situation, she was trying to create "cheat sheets" from handwritten notes taken during her meetings with the sales engineer. That project was slow going, though. The sales engineer discussed the product in a random manner and dismissed many of the competitors she asked him about as minor players.

It seemed to Joelle that every time she went on a sales call, the decision maker appeared to be interested in one of the so called "minor players." Attempts at candor about her lack of product and competitive knowledge, only made the prospect less interested in continuing the conversation. Joelle hoped to have all the necessary product-related facts and information memorized as soon as possible.

JOELLE WILL RECOVER FROM THIS DISASTROUS CALL. IF SHE'S AMBITIOUS, she'll continue to try and put together the product information she needs to answer the customer's questions. Many weeks from today and a few more difficult calls later, everything will fall into place for her.

Experienced sales managers make certain that new hires are ready to address customer objections or give a solid product demo—before they go on the first sales call. This pre-call training gives them confidence and serves as an investment in their future with the company.

Sales and presentation skills are only one part of the equation, however. If sales representatives fumble and stumble when asked questions about their own or a competing product line, a qualified prospect might lose interest. Much of the hard work that went into developing their sales skills will be wasted.

Salespeople need to have excellent command of a lot of different types of information which should include:

> **Presidents who pay little attention to the new hires' overall product and competitive knowledge leave them in a vulnerable position.**

- Product knowledge
- Competitive knowledge
- Frequently asked questions
- Proposal templates
- Company history/facts

PRODUCT KNOWLEDGE

Sales reps accumulate product knowledge by studying marketing materials, using the product or service, working with employees in other departments, learning about the competition, answering customer's questions, and making a few mistakes. In the early days of their tenure most new hires find it difficult to amass product information quickly enough to sound flawlessly credible during a sales call. At the same time, decision-makers expect them—and rightfully so—to know their product or service well.

Product Fact Sheets help to fill gaps between the new rep's knowledge and the decision-maker's expectations. Arranged in an easy-to-follow format, this document contains the basic information a salesperson needs and a prospect is most likely to be interested in during the beginning phases of a sale. Rather than fumbling with handwritten notes or attempting to "make things up as they go along," the new hire can refer to the fact sheet during a sales call and still come across as professional.

Product fact sheets should contain the following:

- Product name
- Description
- Dimensions/specifications/applications
- User profile
- Features
- Benefits
- Perceived market weaknesses
- Competition

Figure 7-1 shows an example of a product fact sheet.

Some new hires worry that referring to any sort of informational sheet reinforces the fact that they are new or gives the appearance they can't be bothered to learn their product. In my experience prospects do not react this way. A fact sheet like this puts important information at the reps' disposal. Both reps and the company they represent look organized and prepared for the sales call.

New hires often express surprise when a prospect sees them referring to a fact sheet and requests a copy for themselves. For this reason, they need to make sure they have extras on hand. No company would want a prospect to see information like perceived market weaknesses and the competition for their own product! To solve this problem, create two versions, one for internal use only and one for the prospective client. These can be posted on the company website as well.

Figure 7-1. Product Fact Sheet

Product	Facts
Product name	Hardy Hammer
Price	$9.99
Description	Wooden handle; steel head; smooth face; curved claw; rubber knob
Dimensions	16 oz. 13" long; 5.5" head
Minimum order	6
Shipping	Standard
Applications	General household repair; driving finish nails
User profile	Homeowners, finish carpenters, trades people
Benefits	Affordable price point Rubber knob decreases handle breakage Manufactured in America Wooden handle preferred by some trades people Smooth face leaves no mark on wood
Perceived market weaknesses	$3 to $5 more expensive than competitors' product Rubber knob drives up cost/serves no real purpose All wooden hammers are alike High costs of American labor
Competition	Envirohammer, Steadyhammer

A well-written fact sheet presents the product or service in a positive but realistic manner. No product can be all things to all people. Regardless of how excited everyone in your company is about the product, the competition will feel otherwise. Be candid about which type of customer the product best serves, and whose needs it can and cannot meet. Point out existing competition and general marketplace perception. Doing anything less than that can put your new hire at a disadvantage when addressing objections or answering questions.

COMPETITIVE DATA

Salespeople hired by large corporations often attend formalized classroom-style sales training before they start calling on clients. This training will likely include a section about the corporation's competitors. The new hires might participate in role playing exercises to practice addressing objections about the competition.

Toward the end of the training module, they might be required to take a test to determine their level of competitive knowledge. When the training ends, the salesperson should know the competitors in their marketplace and understand how to deal with them objectively during a sales call.

In my work with smaller-sized companies, I find that presidents either don't really acknowledge the competition or deal with competing companies in an emotional or angry manner. In some situations the company president is the creator of the product or service and either oblivious or overly sensitive to the fact that there are other like kind products on the market.

Often presidents have a sense of superiority about their "baby" and simply cannot bear to think that another product or service has a feature or two that may indeed trump their own offering. Comments they make about the competition are sometimes harshly critical or dismissive.

Unfortunately, this line of thinking gets transferred to the sales representatives. Not properly educated about their competition, they can appear at worst arrogant or, at best, uninformed when a prospect mentions a competitor during a sales call. Most prospects will listen to a fact-based, professional comparison of competing products. Many will be leery of a sales representative who scoffs at or completely ignores other competitors.

One of my first consulting clients was a company that sold a niche software program to the real estate industry. When I began working with the president, I asked about the competition, and she assured me that there wasn't any. "No product on the market competes with us in terms of price and features," she told me, "We are the only one." I found this surprising but took her at her word—at least initially.

As time went on, I discovered her company had three main competitors. One was considered the top of the line, cost three times what her product did, and had many additional features. This competitor was owned by a large company with vast financial resources. Another competitor sold a scaled-down model that was lower in price and offered fewer features. The third competitor, similar in both cost and features, was owned by a company that produced a variety of niche products for different industries. They were known for their sizable and well-trained sales force.

The hard reality was that my client's sales representatives were losing sales to all three companies on a regular basis. Their reaction to these losses mimicked the president's. They were outraged that their prospect bought an "inferior" product, scoffing at the idea that they had even been in competition with any of these companies to begin with.

Their attitude wasn't confident, it was cocky and misinformed. I knew that for me to be successful, the president had to change her stance toward the competition. If she didn't I wouldn't be able to convince the sales representatives to follow suit.

Knowing full well I was putting my business relationship with her in jeopardy, I met with the president and told her that she had to change her stance about the competition. I went on to say that she had at least three competitors that I knew about and a few I probably didn't know about. These companies produced viable products to which her sales force was losing a considerable number of sales.

I told her the sales representatives might have been able to close some of those sales if they had dealt with the competition in a straightforward and businesslike manner from the beginning. I advised her to equip the sales representatives with competitive fact sheets as well as competitive analysis charts. I added that questions about her competitors had to be added to both the qualifying and the interview questions that the salespeople were asking.

We did not speak for several days. I expected to be paid for my time and quietly asked to move on. But the company president surprised me. Though I know it pained her, she began to open up to me about the competition. Turns out, she knew quite a lot about her competitors and when she began to share this knowledge with me and the sales staff it was a tremendous help.

I gained greater insight as to why she had started her company in the first place and why she priced and positioned her software product the way she had. As a team, we began to assemble the needed information on the competition. The reps enthusiastically researched their assigned competitors and presented their findings at subsequent staff meetings. I knew we'd turned the corner when one of the salespeople made a joke about the competition and the president actually laughed.

It changed the company dynamic and the sales team's attitude substantially. The sales reps went from not asking about their competition at all to having very businesslike feature-by-feature discussions with their prospects. Some sales that might have been lost previously were being closed, which increased everyone's morale and commission checks at the same time.

It all begins when the business executive promotes a healthy and realistic view of the competition as part of company culture.

COMPETITIVE FACT SHEET

Competitive Fact Sheets do everything a product fact sheet does— for a different purpose. It organizes the facts, strong points, and weaknesses of the competitor's product for the new hires. Just as with their own product line, the new reps will have trouble remembering the details about each and every competitor. Referring to a competitive fact sheet enables them to field questions in a businesslike and unemotional manner.

Create a template for the competitive fact sheets and then ask each member of your staff to study a specific competitor. The research could include reviewing the competition's website and marketing materials. They might also discuss the competing product with a company who uses it. If possible—and sometimes it isn't—have them investigate the competition's general pricing.

This project boasts a high success rate. Never once have I asked

Most salespeople do a great job of reporting on competing companies. a sales representative to do research on a particular competitor where he or she hasn't come back to me and said something along the lines of, "You wouldn't believe what I learned about The Colburn Company!" or "In all these years I never knew that Rockland Affiliates was originally started by ...!"

After salespeople complete their homework on the competition, have them fill in a template competitive worksheet with all of the information. Figure 7-2 is an example of a competitive fact sheet for the previously mentioned Hardy Hammer.

A competitive fact sheet presents the competition in an unbiased format. In this example, budget-conscious, eco-friendly customers may gravitate toward the EnviroHammer. Hardware stores, wanting to attract that customer, may be interested in carrying it. The Ridgefield sales representatives must acknowledge the competition (Enviro-Hammer) then make the case for their product (HardyHammer). That's their job.

Have fun with this project. Let the sales reps present their competitive findings at a staff meeting. Ask them to create a short quiz for the salespeople to take afterward. Offer an inexpensive prize for the winner. With the research complete and a fact sheet created for each competitor, into the sales toolkit they go.

For the business executive: get real about your competition. Forget about whom you think you should be competing against or whom you can't believe you have to compete against. Compile a list of those companies you do compete with. Acknowledge the one or two companies that you commonly lose deals to. Make it your business to learn all you can about them and pass this knowledge on to your staff—and most especially—your new hires. Going forward, create a culture that views competitors as a reality of doing business in a free market economy.

FREQUENTLY ASKED QUESTIONS

Salespeople answer questions about their product or service during sales calls. When they can't answer these questions credibly

Figure 7-2. Competitive Fact Sheet

Competitive Product	Facts
Product name	EnviroHammer
Price	$4.95
Description	Bamboo handle; steel head; smooth face; curved claw
Dimensions	16 oz. 13" long, 5.5" head
Minimum order	Case of 48
Shipping	Standard
Applications	General household repair; driving finish nails
User profile	Homeowners, finish carpenters, trades people, environmentally conscious consumers
Benefits	$3–$5 cheaper than competitor Wooden handle "feel" preferred by some trades people Smooth face leaves no mark on wood Handle made from environmentally sustainable materials No extraneous materials
Perceived market weaknesses	No data on bamboo vs. wood for durability Large minimum order Foreign manufacturing Purchase from import/export company Customer service issues
Competition	Hardy Hammer, Steadyhammer

and articulately, or blatantly make up answers, customers sense the lack of basic knowledge and quickly lose interest. A scenario like this can effectively kill a potential sale. New hires frequently suffer from insufficient product knowledge during their initial sales calls. With solid preparation, your sales reps will be ready to field the majority of questions customers ask.

Start the process by asking the current sales staff to write down any and all questions customers ask during sales calls. Though it will be nearly impossible for the sales reps to think of every single question, they will be able to come up with a majority of them, especially the most important ones. Organize these questions by category (such as shipping charges) so that the salesperson can access them quickly during a call.

The frequently asked questions section of the handbook will need to be edited and updated more often than others because of the changing nature of pricing and product or service offerings.

Some examples are as follows:

Figure 7-3. Frequently Asked Questions

Frequently Asked Questions	Response
Does Bronze Level Service include free shipping?	Free shipping is available only with our Gold Level Service.
Can I upgrade before my contract expires?	You can upgrade at any time, paying only the difference between one level of service and another.
Is that available in the color red?	Yes, it's available in red. Let me take out our color chart so that you can look at the other choices, as well.
What is the turnaround time on an order?	Any order placed prior to 2 pm will be sent out that same day.

While a product's color options may not seem important, to a decision-maker who simply must have the color red—it's critical. If your salespeople can quickly and confidently confirm that it does indeed come in that color, they may have an advantage over the competition early on.

Provided the salespeople offer to get back with them in a reasonable period of time, most decision-makers don't mind if there are one or two questions they can't answer. With new salespeople especially, decision-makers will sometimes use their response time to gauge how reactive they are to customer requests. More than a few unanswered questions, though, may test the decision-maker's patience. Avoid putting new hires in this situation by equipping them with the information they need to answer the prospect's inquiries with assurance.

THE PROPOSAL

Part of my work with clients involves a review of their business correspondence. This review always includes the proposal. Over the years, I've noticed a few trends. Most of the proposals I read are long. In addition, my clients put the focus on themselves—their amazing product or service, their knowledgeable and experienced staff, their sincere desire for the prospect's business, and the hard work they will put in if they are chosen. You get the picture.

Generally, little or nothing gets mentioned about the potential client's business, the problems they are hoping to solve, their product requirements, and what they are looking for in a vendor. When I point out to my clients that the proposal should focus first on the prospect and their needs, they are usually taken aback.

For most of them, the idea of making their potential client the focus of the proposal is a new and slightly uncomfortable idea. They had always thought differently. How would they convince a prospect to do business with them if they didn't begin by talking about how fabulous they and their product were? Would they appear as a strong, competitive, and innovative organization? I point out that by opening the proposal with the client's issues instead of theirs, they show themselves to be a customer-oriented, knowledgeable, and competitive business.

> **When writing a proposal, the focus must always be on the client.**

When my clients start putting their prospective customer first in e-mails, product demonstrations, and proposals, they go from feeling uncomfortable to feeling more confident. The salespeople look forward to asking the prospect questions about their needs and goals. They really enjoy crafting the opening paragraph for the proposal. Most rewarding of all, the change sticks. Once companies put their customers ahead of themselves they never go back. It becomes part of their culture. Any sales representative they hire going forward must embrace this idea, as well.

WRITING THE PROPOSAL

Like any written correspondence sent out to customers, proposals cause a lot of difficulties for the new hires and their managers. Sometimes a well-meaning sales manager will say to a new hire, "Our California sales rep Sam writes the best proposals. Ask him to e-mail you one and use that for your new client." New hires do as they are told. Sam e-mails a proposal. So far, so good.

Sam, however, may forward a proposal with information that's outdated or irrelevant to the new hire's potential client. Rather than use Sam's proposal verbatim, the new hires tailor it to more closely match the customer's needs and their personal "style." They may rewrite a paragraph here or delete a clause there.

Unfamiliar with all of the company's policies and procedures, sometimes the information new hires include in the proposal might be flat out wrong. In getting, shall we say, *creative* with the colleague's proposal, the new rep may send out a document not in keeping with the image your company wants to portray.

Like templated correspondence, client proposals should be stan-**dardized to minimize errors and present a consistent look.**

The creation of the sales toolkit is the perfect time to design one or several template proposals. These proposals will have a professional appearance and contain compelling information that will put your organization in a strong position to close the sale. Companies and industries vary in terms of the level of detail necessary for their proposals. Basic sections should include:

- Needs assessment
- Pricing
- Cost-benefit
- Terms of delivery
- Closing statement

Needs Assessment

This opening and all-important section focuses on the clients. Key information includes a brief history of their business, issues of concern to them, and an explanation of how your company's product or service will address these issues.

Pricing

Explanations for all of the costs and charges involved in purchasing from your company are included in this section. Pricing must be straightforward and easily understood. If a company offers several pricing models and the customer has expressed interest in more than one, all models should be included in the proposal.

Cost-Benefit

In this price-conscious era, salespeople must demonstrate the financial value of their product or service. Does the product or service, for example, reduce usage or increase efficiency? If so, demonstrate how either would translate into a tangible savings for the client.

Competitive Analysis

All salespeople put their company in the best light during a sales presentation. So do their competitors. Prospects are sometimes confused as to whose product best fits their needs. A competitive analysis compares the features and benefits of each vendor's product and presents the data in an easy-to-understand format.

Terms of Delivery

Once the customer decides to purchase from your company, when does delivery take place? Is there a product that needs to be installed? Who is responsible for what and when? What costs are involved? All of these details must be included.

Closing Statement

Strong proposals include a closing statement tailored specifically to the prospective client. This final paragraph underscores the benefits of doing business with your organization. It emphasizes your company's sincere desire to enter into a business partnership with the prospect. Here is an example of a proposal.

The Ridgefield Company
25 Maple Lane
Anywhere, USA 12345

Since 1961, independently-owned Three Oaks Hardware has provided high-quality tools to customers in the Magdon County area. A knowledgeable owner and experienced sales staff offer advice to both the homeowner and professional tradesperson.

Competition from large home improvement and hardware store chains makes it critical for Three Oaks to carry a scaled-down inventory with a better-than-average turn. Any item Three Oaks carries must be competitively priced and of superior quality.

For that reason, The Ridgefield Co. recommends that Three Oaks Hardware carry the HardyHammer for its price point and durability. The HardyHammer will appeal to those customers needing tools for simple home repair jobs and for the tradesperson who prefers the "feel" of a wooden-handled hammer for finish work.

Pricing

Three Oaks estimates sales of 4 hammers per month, or 48 annually. Based on this, they would order 9 times per year at 6 hammers per order for a total of 54 hammers per year.

One Hammer

Retail Price	Cost	Markup	Gross Margin	Profit
$9.99	$4.00	150%	60%	$5.99

Single Order (6 hammers)

Retail Price	Cost	Profit	Shipping Chgs.
$59.94	$24.00	$35.94	$4.98

Annual Order

Retail Price	Cost	Profit	Shipping Chgs.
$539.46	$216.00	$323.46	$ 44.82

9 Boxes of 6 (54 Hammers)

To select a hammer, Three Oaks Hardware will be choosing among three vendors:

Hammer	Vendor
HardyHammer	The Ridgefield Company
EnviroHammer	Enviro Corporation
SteadyHammer	Telmar Distribution

Comparison of the three vendors based on the purchase of a single hammer is as follows:

Hammer	Retail Price	Markup	Gross Margin	Profit
HandyHammer	$9.99	150%	60%	$5.99
EnviroHammer*	$4.95	153%	60%	$3.00
SteadyHammer*	$5.49	150%	60%	$3.29

*Based on industry estimates

The following table compares profitability among the three vendors, assuming annual sales of 48 hammers:

Hammer	Retail Price	Cost	Profit
HandyHammer	$479.52	$192.00	$287.52
EnviroHammer	$237.60	$93.60	$144.00
SteadyHammer	$263.52	$105.60	$157.92

Competitive Analysis

Hammer	Inventory Turn	Minimum Order	SPIF Program	U.S.-Based Cust. Svc.
HandyHammer	8	6 pcs	Yes	Yes
EnviroHammer*	1	48 (case)	No	No
SteadyHammer*	1	52 (case)	No	No

The HardyHammer offers the following advantages to the cost-conscious business owner:
- More profitable than competitors
- Ability to order on an as needed basis
- No extra inventory to store
- Independent durability testing
- Price point under $10
- Direct sales force

Red Tag SPIF Program

Twice annually (March and August), The Ridgefield Co. sponsors our very popular Red Tag SPIF program. Bright red hanging tags offering $2 off the Hardy Hammer are sent to participating retailers. Attached to the tags are clear boxes containing samples from our nail line (usually finishing or panel nails).

Consumers receive $2 off when they purchase the hammer, and the Ridgefield sales representative handles reimbursement for the retailer. It's the simplest SPIF program in the industry.

Terms of Delivery

On approval of the credit application and the receipt of the signed contract, the first shipment of six (6) HardyHammers will be sent by standard delivery (3–5 business days).

Since 1948, The Ridgefield Company has been offering top-quality building materials to hardware retailers. The knowledge and experience of our 271-person sales force is unrivaled in the industry.

At Ridgefield we understand the needs of a locally owned hardware store like Three Oaks and will work with you and your staff to ensure we offer the high quality and competitively priced merchandise that your store will be proud to carry.

Thank you for considering The Ridgefield Company as your hardware provider. I will call you on July 10 at 9:00 am to discuss our next step.

> Sincerely,
> Sam Salesperson
> Account Sales Representative
> The Ridgefield Company

THE IMPORTANCE OF THE COST-BENEFIT SECTION

Most of my clients understand how to explain the pricing of their product or service in the proposal. They do a good job of presenting the different pricing options in an easy-to-understand and visually attractive format. The area in which they typically falter, at least where the financial data is concerned, occurs in the presentation of the Cost-Benefit or the ROI (return on investment). Many companies make a half-hearted attempt at including a cost-benefit section in the proposal. Others leave it out altogether.

A correlation exists between the lack of a cost-benefit section and the president's strong feelings about the competition. Sales representatives may worry that acknowledging or comparing the product or service to that of their competitors could potentially result in falling out of favor with the president. For this reason they might avoid approaching a department like finance to assist them in creating a strong ROI comparison chart. Other sales representatives may not even be aware of the value of the cost-benefit section to a professional sales proposal.

Acting confidently, believing in your product, and answering questions accurately all greatly increase the chances of closing a sale. In terms of pricing, your product does not even need to be the cheapest one on the market, necessarily. In a highly competitive environment, which most companies find themselves in, the responsibility rests with you to prove that your product or service offers financial advantages over the others your prospect may be considering.

In the sample proposal, HardyHammer sells for $9.99. The EnviroHammer and the SteadyHammer sell for $4.95 and $5.49, respectively. It should be an easy decision for Three Oaks Hardware, right? Buy one of the cheaper hammers and make the customer happy. But guess what? It's slightly more complicated than that. The HardyHammer offers $129 and $143 more in profit than their two closest competitors. Aren't they in business to make money? In addition, Ridgefield offers Three Oaks the ability to order six hammers at a time. With EnviroHammer, as an example, they must order 48 all at once. Why hold that amount of inventory for the better part of a year?

Besides greater profitability and attractive shipping options, The Ridgefield Company offers a rebate program, a well-trained sales force, and product quality testing. They should be proud of all of this and have every right to include it in their proposal. Before any of that is mentioned, though, they walk their customer through the financial incentives of doing business with them. They prove their case in dollars and cents.

Many of my clients initially balk at having to create an ROI. They say to me, "I sell the same stuff as Joe two towns over. There is no price difference. It's all about making sure the items are always in stock and being able to deliver them on time!"

Because the majority of sales representatives lack access to all the necessary financial data and may not have the math skills to assemble one on their own, the appropriate parties in your organ- **ization must work as a team to put together an easy-to-understand ROI.**

If your organization sells a commoditized product and the strength of your proposal rests on your ability to service your customer—so be it. But you must demonstrate how this high-quality customer service helps the customer save money in the long run. They, in turn, must be able to understand the explanation and agree with it!

Having the ability to present a customer with thorough and believable ROI data gives all sales reps an added boost of self-confidence. Not every company bothers with this type of information. Be the one that does. It puts you a step ahead of the competition.

FINAL THOUGHTS ON THE PROPOSAL

In looking at this proposal, you may be thinking, "This Ridgefield Co. would never go to the trouble of writing a proposal for 48 hammers." And you would be right. Undoubtedly, the Ridgefield sales representative would propose that Three Oaks Hardware carry a much broader inventory (nails, screwdrivers, and saws, to name but a few). For the purposes of this chapter, I wanted to present a product everyone could relate to (hammers) and emphasize format and presentation. To achieve this I had the Ridgefield Co. propose only one product.

Your sales staff has probably been writing and sending out proposals of one form or another for years. Some sales reps may be very set in their ways, while others are open to considering a new way of writing one. Have everyone bring their ideas to the table and design a top-rate proposal that puts the potential client first while still showcasing what your company has to offer.

COMPANY HISTORY

Many potential land mines await the poor beleaguered new sales representative. If they aren't worried about making a mistake during their presentation, they're apprehensive about answering an FAQ incorrectly. With all of this to concern themselves with, most give little thought to the history of the company they work for. Rarely does anyone at the company put any effort into educating them on this subject. This lack of company knowledge is usually a fairly benign situation until a customer or prospect makes reference to past business dealings with the company (good or bad).

If the new hires look clueless when these prior transactions are mentioned, the prospect's interpretation might be that they didn't do their homework before the sales call. If a serious problem has occurred between the two companies and the new rep pleads ignorance, the customer may think the new hire isn't interested in hearing about something that occurred before his or her time. Those customers who have been buying products or services from a company for a considerable period of time will expect the new hire to thank them for their business and acknowledge the long-term relationship between the two organizations. When this doesn't happen, they may take offense.

Let me share a story with you.

A salesperson I knew many years ago, once called on a department store buyer who said to her, "How's my buddy Tommy?"

"Tommy?" she asked.

"Your company president?"

"Oh, yeah. Right. Of course. Thomas Grant. He's great. Do you two know each other?" she answered awkwardly.

"Know each other? That's a good one. Many years back, I was the assistant manager of a long-ago closed store. He used to drive the delivery truck for his dad, who was the president in those days. My store was on his route. I'm surprised he didn't mention all of this to you."

Tommy, the young man that drove the delivery truck, was now the mature, polished company president who had asked to be called Thomas. The buyer was a little bit cool toward this sales representative after she realized the rep knew nothing of her prior professional relationship with him. The whole conversation left the sales representative feeling disconcerted.

When the new rep mentioned the sales call to "Tommy," he gave her an odd look and then said, "Please set up a meeting for the two of us to go see her."

A week or two later, the rep and Thomas Grant went to see the buyer. The two of them seemed genuinely glad to see each other. She chided him for not coming to see her for so long. He apologized. They talked a little business, told a few war stories, and caught up on the whereabouts of former colleagues. Nothing eventful went on one way or another. The rep knows that there was probably a back-story she wasn't privy to. However, her own relationship with the buyer was greatly improved during subsequent sales calls.

After reading this story, some of you might be thinking, "That's unfair. The buyer shouldn't hold it against a rep because the president neglected to tell her that he used to drive his dad's delivery truck!" Fair? Maybe not. Realistic? Very.

This buyer wanted her long relationship with the company acknowledged. Maybe she felt that because she'd known him since he was very young, Mr. Grant owed her the occasional personal visit. Whether or not her expectations were reasonable, she was the customer.

At the very least, Thomas Grant should have shared the history of the two companies with the sales representative and asked her to say hello to the buyer personally. By not doing so, he put his sales representative in a difficult and uncomfortable position.

Prospects are always looking for excuses not to buy or a way to test a new rep. Don't give them more ammunition. Add a section on the history of your company to the training toolkit and make sure you share a few stories with the new hire at some point during new hire orientation.

This section of the toolkit should contain information on:

- Early days of the company
- Original owners/partners
- First few customers
- Customers of longstanding
- Companies purchased/sold/merged
- Former office locations
- Additional factories or office buildings
- Product lines (present and former)

As in the example with Thomas Grant, some historical information will pertain only to certain customers in specific sales territories. Sit down with new hires and talk with them about the customers they will be meeting. Some of the details you might want to share could include:

- Long-standing client relationships
- Past clients
- Favors done in the past
- Win-win business deals
- Business mishaps
- Special contract terms
- Difficult client relationships

Knowledge of company history benefits all employees, but new hires have the most to gain. They are out meeting customers all the time. Knowing the origins of your business and understanding how the various client relationships evolved will help them establish a stronger bond with their new customers more more quickly.

COMPLETING THE TOOLKIT

In reading this chapter, you may feel that I have omitted certain types of information that might benefit a salesperson in your organization. Some of the subjects that I suggested for inclusion in the toolkit may not be relevant to your company. Customize your binder so that it contains what your salespeople need to increase their chances for success.

Other sections you can add might include:

- Price list
- Gross profit calculations
- Sample customer contract
- Negotiating guidelines

Certain sections of the handbook that you and your staff worked so hard to create will become outdated in a few months' time (painful but true). Someone at the company must be put in charge of keeping the handbook up-to-date at least two times a year and sending updates to the salespeople. The salespeople must be responsible for incorporating these updates. Whether they are keeping their toolkit current should be noted during the performance review process.

If someone within your company has an aptitude for graphic

design, let this person add to the overall look of the toolkit. If there happens to be a talented writer on staff, perhaps you could ask that employee to edit the final version for clarity and punctuation. Where these skills aren't available in-house, you might want to look into outsourcing that type of work.

When I put a toolkit together for a company, I go to a printer and have customized tabs made for the hard copy. I find those tabs add a finished and professional look. No matter what you decide to do from a style standpoint, the toolkit does not have to be elaborate. Only the contents truly matter. The toolkit will be a valuable resource for your entire sales staff for years to come.

8

Setting
Realistic Goals

Kurt really enjoyed his conversation with Maureen, the new salesperson. She was telling him about a cold call she made to a decision maker that resulted in an appointment for the following week. She seemed excited and Kurt, the company president, was glad for her.

The next day, he looked at the daily activity report and saw that she had made only five outbound calls the entire day. Five! Was she kidding?? He thought she should be making a whole lot more than that. And one appointment?? If she had any hope of making quota, he knew she would have to step up her efforts considerably.

Kurt feels Maureen, an experienced salesperson, should know her productivity is unacceptably low. Has he made a disastrous hire? He's upset and she needs to know about it. Five calls a day indeed!

THE DISCUSSION BETWEEN KURT AND MAUREEN PROBABLY WON'T GO SO well. On a high from her successful prospecting call, she'll feel quickly deflated when Kurt lights into her. He may be justified in wanting her to make more calls. No matter how many more she makes, though, if she had no idea how many to make to begin with, she'll feel unfairly criticized.

Maureen could be feeling pretty good about her cold calling. It may have taken her all day to make those five calls. Between experimenting with her introduction and finding the answers to customers' questions, Maureen may feel that she did the best she could. Kurt won't know about this. He'll be too aggravated to ask.

FINDING THE RIGHT NUMBER

How many prospecting calls should new salespeople be expected to make in their first month? How many appointments should they reasonably be expected to go on during their first business quarter? When should a new sales representative really be expected to start selling? Anyone charged with managing a sales force has struggled with these questions again and again.

Because they aren't sure how to set appropriate goals for the new hire, some business executives like Kurt avoid setting any at all. The lack of clearly defined objectives leads to frustration and misunderstandings on both sides. No one formula exists for setting these goals—they vary by industry, product, the salesperson's skills, and so on. But that shouldn't stop you from establishing milestones and goals for the new sales representative.

All salespeople, regardless of tenure, need targets to add focus and discipline to their day.

GETTING STARTED

Every product or service has a sales cycle. Typically, it starts with the introduction and proceeds through to the close of the sale. In general, the steps are:

- Introduction or prospecting call
- Conversation with decision-maker
- Appointment
- Product demonstration or proof of capabilities
- Proposal
- Closed sale

The vast majority of sales opportunities pass through these stages. Your company's sales cycle may have a few more or one less step than the one I show. Some sort of process or cycle exists for your product or service. People often compare these stages to a funnel. Salespeople need to generate a lot of potential opportunities in the beginning to ensure they have enough prospects to close at the end.

Some salespeople make prospecting or cold calls as a way to introduce themselves and their company to decision-makers. Others try to establish contact through referrals from other customers or colleagues in their professional network. Many follow-up on leads from trade shows or advertising sponsored by their company. Most sales representatives use a combination of those approaches.

No matter how they come into contact with the decision-maker, only a percentage of conversations will result in a second conversation or appointment. Some number of those conversations or appointments will convert to decision-makers agreeing to see a product demonstration or presentation. After watching a product demo or presentation, a fraction of those prospects will be interested enough to ask for a proposal. Once a salesperson has submitted a proposal, he or she knows that one in every so many proposals will result in a closed sale.

Within the sales cycle a sales representative will do a tremendous amount of work including: placing follow-up phone calls or e-mails, making additional presentations to different groups, answering innumerable questions, and participating in pre-proposal discussions. Some potential sales opportunities languish at one stage for a long time or skip through a particular stage rapidly. Whatever your sales cycle looks like, use it as the basis for creating the appropriate productivity goals.

> **The length of a sales cycle can vary from a single phone call, to several months, to more than a year.**

SETTING PRODUCTIVITY GOALS

So what's the best way for a business executive to create goals for the new salesperson? If minimum productivity goals already exist for your sales organization, take those goals and divide them into thirds. For the first month the new hire should be expected to make one-third as many prospecting calls, for instance, as a tenured representative. During the second month the new rep should make two-thirds as many, and during the third month the rep should be at 90% or greater of the required minimum productivity goals.

Let's say that the weekly, monthly, and quarterly goals for a tenured salesperson are as follows:

Figure 8-1. Current Productivity Goals

	Month	Week	Day
Prospecting Calls	500	125	25
Conversations	40	10	2
Appointments	16	4	0
Product Demonstrations	12	3	0
Proposals	8	2	0
Closed Sales	4	1	0

Set the goals for the new hire as follows:

Figure 8-2. New Hire Productivity Goals

Productivity Goals: Month One			
	Month	Week	Day
Prospecting Calls	167	42	8
Conversations	14	4	1
Appointments	5	1	0
Product Demonstrations	4	1	0
Proposals	2	1	0
Closed Sales	1	0	0

Figure 8-2. New Hire Productivity Goals (continued)

Productivity Goals: Month Two			
	Month	**Week**	**Day**
Prospecting Calls	300	75	15
Conversations	24	6	1
Appointments	10	3	1
Product Demonstrations	7	2	0
Proposals	3	1	0
Closed Sales	2	1	0
Productivity Goals: Month Three			
	Month	**Week**	**Day**
Prospecting Calls	450	113	23
Conversations	36	9	2
Appointments	14	4	1
Product Demonstrations	11	3	1
Proposals	7	2	0
Closed Sales	3	1	0

On Day One new hires understand what you expect, and it changes the way they approach the job. A confusing, demoralizing conversation, like the one Kurt will have with Maureen doesn't need to occur.

If new hires have trouble hitting their scaled-down goals, the conversation can be constructive and specific. A president might say, "I see that your prospecting call numbers are strong but you seem to be struggling to make the minimum number of appointments. Let's talk about that. I'd like to help in any way I can." The president asks, listens, coaches, and offers assistance as opposed to assuming and lecturing.

LACK OF DATA

Dividing the new hire's goals into thirds might seem to make sense—if you actually have goals to divide. But what if you don't? What if you have no idea what your average sales representative's daily activity level is? How do you proceed? This task is especially difficult if there have *never* been any productivity goals set for any of the sales staff, which often happens in smaller companies.

Do your best to determine what your sales cycle looks like. Talk to the reps and those who work in other departments to see if your thinking is in line with how they see the sales cycle. Then ask your current sales staff to start tracking their related activities. If you have a sales software system, have them log their activities as they go through the work day. If you don't use a sales software system currently—and many companies do not—give your sales staff a worksheet and have them track their activities with old-fashioned tick marks.

Companies use a variety of programs like ACT! or Salesforce.com to track their sales data. I refer to sales software generically, using the term sales software system.

After a few weeks, run the numbers. Find out, for instance, how many prospecting calls your top sales representative makes in a week. How many does the lowest-performing salesperson make? What is the average for the group? What number of appointments do they go on each week? How many proposals do they send out? Work your way through the sales cycle and answer all of those questions.

When business executives do this exercise, their reactions vary from surprised to greatly displeased. Many find the low levels of activity alarming They're upset with themselves for not paying more attention. Regardless of how they feel, what they have at the end of this exercise are the facts about their sales staff's activity level and a starting point from which to begin thinking about the appropriate productivity goals for the new hire.

But what if a business executive now knows that the sales staff isn't making the number of calls that they could or should? Do they use those low productivity numbers as a basis for the new sales representative's goals or disregard them altogether and start with new goals?

> **I remind my clients** that even disappointing information is more and better information than they've ever had before.

These are good questions. If the current numbers are low, increase them by a small percentage, then divide the new numbers into thirds for the new hire. As unsatisfactory as they may be, do use the current staff's numbers as a baseline. You can always increase the productivity requirements for the new hires during months two and three based on their performance.

As for your current staff, you will have a better chance of successfully improving their performance going forward if you increase their productivity goals gradually (say, by 10–20% per month for a three- to six-month period). Don't surprise them. Discuss the issue of increasing the goals before the new hire begins.

NO STAFF

What happens in a case where a company is hiring their first salesperson ever or has not had a salesperson on staff for a long time? What if they have no data to rely on whatsoever? Call professional organizations in your industry. Speak to peers with like businesses in other areas of the country. Ask about the productivity goals that they set. Meet with local area business people, regardless of industry, and get a general picture of what they require from their sales representatives.

Let go of thinking that your goals have to be perfect or you can't set them at all. Use a combination of research, information from other business people, and your solid instincts. Remember, no goal has to be permanent and they are always adjustable.

UNDER-/OVER-PERFORMING

Sometimes, especially when a business executive attempts to set productivity goals for the first time, the new salesperson either blows the goals away or falls short of achieving them. This upsets most business executives. When it happens to my clients, I congratulate them for trying to set goals in the first place. I then ask them if they truly regret the attempt, even if the numbers did not work out perfectly the first time. Surprisingly, they always say, "No, I don't regret it at all. It was a huge learning experience, and I feel like I am getting closer to knowing what the goals should actually be."

So what do you do if new sales reps are either way over or way under where they need to be with regard to productivity? Perhaps they're trying to impress you and are calling at a pace they can't possibly maintain over time. Maybe their numbers are over or under in one or two categories, but more in line with the goals set in others. Could exceeding the required number of conversations and product demonstrations make up for lower numbers than you would like to see?

Have a chat with the reps. Ask them these questions and any others that may be appropriate. Strategize together on determining a new set of goals. They should want to work with you on setting the numbers accurately. They know it will benefit them financially if the goals motivate them to reach and stretch a bit.

IRONIES IN SALES

Anyone in sales knows that one morning you can make 100 prospecting calls and not have a conversation with a single prospect. On another morning you can get through to someone almost immediately. Sales can be unpredictable, aggravating, and exciting—all in the span of a day or two. Targets and objectives help sales representatives with the ups and downs involved in the sales profession.

Take the time to set reasonable productivity goals and tailor them to new hires. Discuss these goals before their first day on the job. Let them know that there are definite expectations starting on Day One. Those not committed to sales or not money-motivated will find this threatening. Those sales representatives who want to be successful will find this very helpful and use the goals to their advantage.

9

Calling on the Largest Accounts

Adam feels sick over the whole situation. He wants desperately to fix things. But with Regina, the company president, in such a rage he can't go to her for advice.

After he had been with the company a few weeks, Regina asked him to visit his top accounts before the end of the month. Adam asked her administrative assistant to run a list of the largest accounts in his territory.

Instead of running a list of his top accounts for last year, the administrative assistant handed him a list of the top accounts year-to-date. He began to contact and visit them one by one. The Telken Corporation wasn't on the list. In fact, their gross sales revenue Y-T-D didn't even put them in the top half of the companies in his territory.

Unbeknownst to Adam, Telken was his fifth largest account, but they placed only a few orders a year. Worse yet, all of the orders get placed in the last quarter of the year. After Adam had been with the company for two months, the president of Telken called Regina to discuss how disappointed she was that the new sales representative couldn't be bothered to stop by. The president also added that Telken was in the process of putting the order out to bid.

REGINA'S COMPANY MAY LOSE TELKEN'S BUSINESS. ADAM AND REGINA'S still-new working relationship has been badly shaken. Even if

Telken agrees to continue as a client, they may ask to have Adam removed as the sales representative. Problems abound where a previously strong alliance existed between the two companies.

Before new hires join an organization, a business executive needs to put a strategy in place for having them assume responsibility for the accounts in their territory. More importantly, they must have a plan for the largest of these accounts.

Transferring major accounts to the new salesperson represents a critical step for most companies— and it often goes awry.

The process of reassigning major accounts to a new rep indicates how valued clients are treated at your company. Did you give clients any advance notice about the change in sales representatives? Were they informed by e-mail or phone call? Will you be accompanying the new rep on the first call? Will the clients be communicated with at all during this interim period?

During the first sales call, clients observe new sales representatives. How do they conduct themselves? Are they nervous and fumbling or poised and prepared? How do they deal with an awkward question such as, "what happened to the sales representative who used to call on us?" Do they have a system for handling problems? Sales reps need to be aware that their actions are being judged.

COMPETITORS

Presidents can forget that in failing to plan for their largest accounts, they unwittingly leave some space for their competitors. Once other vendors hear about the change in sales representatives, they will capitalize on the situation. A new, unproven sales representative offers a potential window of opportunity to penetrate the account.

A client may have experienced problems with your company in the past. Paradoxically, they might have received superior service from your former sales representative. The client will wonder what level of professionalism and attention to detail the new salesperson will provide. If any doubt exists, a competitor will make a strong case for your client to switch vendors.

Businesses of all sizes must understand that 20% of their accounts are probably responsible for 80% of their sales revenue. It's even more critical for a small business to grasp this concept. Fewer accounts make up that vital 20%. Every reasonable measure needs to be taken to retain their business. There aren't as many customers to spread the risk over.

Before the new salesperson starts, four decisions need to be made regarding the transfer of major accounts:

1. What information the new salesperson needs to have prior to the first call
2. Which employee will communicate with the account during the interim
3. Who will introduce the new sales representative to the accounts
4. When that initial introduction/sales call will be made

ACCOUNT INFORMATION

A well-balanced new hire orientation includes having the new rep spend time learning about and preparing to meet the largest accounts.

They should conduct their own research using a combination of the Internet, press releases, trade journal articles, and annual reports. Looking only at their customer's website will give the sales representative biased information—and that's not considered research. Additional exploration should include speaking directly to people in your company who work closely with the account (for example, customer service) and reviewing all relevant sales data.

Sometimes new hires spend an inordinate amount of time learning about their major accounts. Exhaustive research is overkill. They aren't writing a thesis. I tell my clients they'll know new hires have completed the project when they are able to "tell a story" about the account in plain business English. To tell a credible story, the following information should be included about each client:

- Years in business
- Public/private/family-owned
- Understanding of company history
- Major products/services offered
- Main competitors
- General state of the industry
- Sales history
- Business relationships with others in new hire's company

A great story might sound something like this:

Using their middle names for the business they started together, brothers Arnold Jackson Carswell and Joseph Finch Carswell founded Jackson & Finch. Since 1962, they have provided office supplies to businesses in the greater Houston area. The office supply industry has always been very competitive with everyone from drug stores to convenience markets selling pens, pencils, and notebooks. Their willingness to deliver office supplies to both large and small companies helped set them apart.

In the early 1980s they expanded their business to include the repair of computers and printers. They also began to carry an inventory of hard-to-find parts for older office machinery. This expansion of their business combined with the economic recession in the early 1980s led to some difficult times financially. They talked to our company about their situation and worked out payment arrangements for overdue invoices.

Jackson & Finch compete with a national office supply franchise and two independent local office equipment repair companies. They have been a client of our company for more than a decade with gross sales of $35,000 in 2007. For many years, they purchased only Product C but started to purchase Product B in 2004. Arnie and Joe remain active in the business, pay their bills in a timely fashion, and are two of the toughest negotiators in the office supply industry."

REVENUE HISTORY

No research can be considered complete unless the new hire understands:

- Which products major accounts buy
- The amount of each product they purchase

Figure 9-1. Major Account Sales Revenue

Customer	2006	2007	2008	2009	2010	Total	'09 vs '10	5-yr Avg
Smyth Company	$16,000	$14,000	$13,000	$12,000	$9,000	$64,000	-25%	$12,800
Marbeth Assoc.	$7,000	$30,000	$32,000	$36,000	$37,000	$142,000	3%	$28,400
Jackson & Finch	$18,000	$23,000	$27,000	$30,000	$35,000	$133,000	17%	$26,600
Fallston Corp.	$11,000	$39,000	$19,000	$22,000	$25,000	$116,000	14%	$23,200
The Manlen Co.	$31,000	$37,000	$44,000	$48,000	$46,000	$206,000	-4%	$41,200
Totals	$83,000	$143,000	$135,000	$148,000	$152,000	$661,000	3%	$132,200

If this type of information is relatively easy to find, let new hires handle it themselves. If it's difficult to access, ask them to work in tandem with someone or provide them with the information. A major account report looks something like Figure 9-1.

This report speaks volumes. A salesperson will immediately see, for instance, sales to the Smyth Company have been declining steadily since 2003 but that the decline has been gradual. They will wonder why. Marbeth Associates, on the other hand, started out purchasing a modest $7,000 in 2003 and now only the Manlen Company brings in more sales revenue. What accounts for that impressive increase?

Reports that break sales revenue down by product. Figure 9-2 provides some of those answers.

When new sales representatives look at this report, they will see that sales for the Smyth Company declined by 25% for the year, consistently, through-

Figure 9-2. Major Account Sales by Product

	2006	%	2007	%	2008	%	2009	%	2010	%
Smyth Company	$16,000	%	$14,000	%	$13,000	%	$12,000	%	$9,000	%
Product A	$4,300	27%	$5,000	36%	$8,300	40%	$5,900	49%	$4,700	52%
Product B	$2,900	18%	$2,600	19%	$2,700	13%	$1,600	13%	$900	10%
Product C	$8,800	55%	$6,400	46%	$10,000	48%	$4,500	38%	$3,400	38%
Marbeth Assoc.	$7,000	%	$30,000	%	$32,000	%	$36,000	%	$37,000	%
Product A	—	0%	$5,000	17%	$4,400	12%	$4,700	13%	$5,000	14%
Product B	—	0%	—	0%	—	0%	—	9%	—	0%
Product C	$7,000	100%	$25,000	83%	$31,600	88%	$31,300	87%	$32,000	86%
Jackson & Finch	$18,000	%	$23,000	%	$27,000	%	$30,000	%	$35,000	%
Product A	—	27%	—	0%	—	0%	—	0%	—	0%
Product B	—	18%	$3,000	13%	$5,000	19%	$4,000	13%	$6,000	17%
Product C	$18,000	55%	$20,000	87%	$22,000	81%	$26,000	87%	$29,000	83%

out each product line. The new sales rep will note that Marbeth Associates' sales revenue increased by 3% for the year and they have never purchased Product B. This makes their purchase of Products A and C all the more important. Jackson & Finch is up 17% for the year and more than 80% of their purchases are generated by Product C. Ambitious, money-motivated salespeople will make interesting observations and ask challenging questions.

Once new hires have had a chance to review reports like these, meet with them and answer their questions. Encourage their curiosity. Tell them a few "war stories" about each account. Most company owners or presidents know quite a bit about the larger clients and might have had a hand in signing them as customers. Discussing this group of valued clients with the new hire will influence the new person positively.

For new hire orientation, use my suggested reports along with others of importance to your organization. During the first sales call, larger accounts are unlikely to quiz the new hire about revenue levels from three years ago. They might have to look up the information themselves! But they probably will ask the rep a few questions to gauge his or her overall knowledge of their company. The new hire will simply feel more confident knowing that he or she won't appear totally unprepared during the first meeting.

SPEAKING TO THE RELEVANT PLAYERS

Encourage new hires to have discussions with the employees in the company who interact with the larger clients on a regular basis. Departments such as customer service, shipping, and accounts payable know how a particular account likes to be dealt with. Customer service may have some insight into who makes most of the decisions and who influences them. Accounts payable knows whether they pay their bills on time and what recent problems might have occurred.

Allow people from other departments to speak the truth about these top accounts. If one complains loudly about reasonable price increases—so be it. If another places their order at the last minute and demands overnight shipping at ground shipping prices—let that be known. New sales representatives needn't confront the top accounts with this information. They should simply feel more knowledgeable about these all important customers.

HANDLING THE ACCOUNT

During the period of time when they aren't being called on by a sales representative, someone from your company needs to communicate with the largest accounts. If the president has a previous relationship, perhaps he or she can assume the responsibility. If someone in customer service has a solid connection with them, that person could take over the duty for a time.

Regardless of who does what, the account should not be ignored. Someone should pick up the phone and speak with them. Let the customer know what's going to happen. The conversation might sound something like this:

> This is Paul President with the Stafford Company. Betty Jones has been calling on you for the past several years. She's moving on to another opportunity, and I am in the process of hiring a new sales representative to take her place. In the meantime, Ed Brown, whom you know from customer service, will be the main contact for your account. He'll be calling you later today. So, how are things with everyone there …

This call should be looked on as a terrific opportunity to chat with a valued account. Customers always appreciate the gesture, yet few business owners make the effort. Many let the account go unmanaged until they've hired a new sales representative. Then they let the new hire call the account and explain the change. Bad business practices like this can open the door for the competition.

When working with *my* clients, I encourage them to pick up the phone and have this conversation with *their* clients. I have gotten pushback over the years. Presidents tell me that they avoid making the call because they might get stuck having to do a lot of work for the account. Others worry that once they do hire a new sales representative they will have difficulty extricating themselves from handling the account. Some are concerned that calling the client to discuss the change in sales representatives will lead the client to think they are mismanaging their business and experiencing high turnover within the sales organization as a result. The excuses go on and on.

I advise (insist, cajole, nag) them to make these calls. Afterward most sheepishly admit that it wasn't nearly as awful as they imagined. In the majority of cases, the clients enjoyed hearing from them. Many learn how their organization is perceived. Most of the perceptions are positive. All acknowledge that calling their largest accounts from time to time should become part of their regular routine.

INTRODUCING THE SALES REPRESENTATIVE

When the new salesperson starts work, call these valued clients and tell them about the person you've chosen to handle their accounts. If the salesperson has a large number of customers in their territory, you might want to notify some of them by way of a letter or an e-mail. But communicate with the top accounts either in person or by phone.

If your organization *has* had a problem with turnover in the sales force, address the situation. The client might be skeptical about having to meet another new rep. Your call should acknowledge the turnover and outline what you're doing to improve the situation. Don't let your competitors tell them that you will be hiring *yet another* sales representative. What could be worse than that?

Why? Why should *you* have to do this? The people in your company's largest accounts are grown-ups. They've seen salespeople come and go. What's all the fuss about? Well, the fuss is about the success of your business. Yes, your accounts have had any number of salespeople call on them over the years—some great and some not so good. Yes, they've always survived the change of personnel.

By taking the time to personally introduce your salesperson, you reinforce with the client how much you value their business. As president, communicate that *you* selected this new person, *you* are confident in this person's capabilities; and that *you* are making sure the new rep has the appropriate training before *you* send him or her on a call. Promise the client that *you* will work closely with the new hire to ensure that the client receives the time and attention that they deserve.

> Anytime a new salesperson takes over, an account will always wonder if they will be well taken care of.

The phone call might start out something like this:

This is Paul President with the Stafford Company. I hired a salesperson named Ruth Thomas as your new account representative. She starts this coming Monday, but we're going to keep her around the office for a few weeks so she can learn our product line. She has sold copiers in the past, so she should have an understanding of that side of your business. I asked Ed Brown to keep in contact with your account while we hired a new sales rep. Has he been calling you regularly? In about three weeks or so, I'll have Ruth give you a call, so both she and I can come out and meet with you. How does that work for you?

A lot has been accomplished here: you've told your customer about the new salesperson, provided some information about her background, ensured they were taken care of in the interim, and informed them about the next step. In doing so, you stand behind your salesperson and show respect for your client.

Surprise, surprise, many of the company presidents that I work with balk at making this call, as well. They say things like, "The salesperson should call and introduce himself [herself]," or "I don't have time to accompany them on all their sales calls—that's why I hired them." Others will admit that they want to avoid looking foolish. "What if this person doesn't work out?" They'll ask me. "Will I have gone to all this trouble just to look like an idiot?"

They're missing the point. This isn't about them and how they will look. We're talking about making the extra effort for an account that spends a lot of money with their company. The gesture demonstrates sensitivity toward the *account* and how *they* feel.

Don't make a decision (such as not accompanying your sales representative on the first sales call) based on *potential* failure. Assume a positive outcome. Should the salesperson not work out for whatever reason, communicate with the client in a candid and professional manner when the time comes.

THE FIRST SALES CALL

Anyone with sales experience has heard a salesperson's first round of introductory calls. They sound something like:

This is Ruth Thomas with the Stafford Company. I'm your new

rep and I was just calling to touch base. Can I help you with anything today? OK, great. Let me give you my contact information so you can call me for anything you might need.

A similar situation plays out with field sales representatives. Sometimes they "just drop by" without an appointment and leave their card (often with a disinterested office manager or employee who just happened to be walking by). Some reps go on an initial call without an agenda, awkwardly introducing themselves to the busy and ambivalent decision-maker before quickly leaving.

Regrettably, whether in person or by phone, most new reps go into their first call with a valued customer unprepared. The new hire may see the first call as useful or necessary. In reality, everyone's time has been wasted.

The damage may be minimal when conversations or visits like these take place in smaller accounts. It's another matter altogether if the first call to a major account gets handled this way. Though well-meaning, the new hire could come across as disorganized or amateurish. The account could find the drop-by visit or impromptu phone call rude or a nuisance and wonder why the salesperson bothered.

Calls to major accounts require pre-planning and organization. The company president should either accompany the new salespeople or join them on the call by teleconference (or whatever technology is available). Most calls work best when the president makes some introductory comments and then *turns the call over* to the sales representative.

To prevent this client visit from turning into a "just thought I'd call and introduce myself" waste of time, the salesperson needs two things: a list of questions and something to offer the client or tell them about.

THE LIST OF QUESTIONS

If the new salespeople have done their due diligence, they know a fair amount about the account they are calling on (which you should verify yourself by quizzing them about the company before your visit). Good salespeople will arrive at the call with a list of prepared questions underscoring how organized, informed, and eager they are to learn about this new account. The questions that get asked on the first call should never take on the feel of an interrogation, but rather one of curiosity and a desire to better understand the account.

A list of questions could include:

- I understand from my research and talking with Paul President that your company specializes in (products/services) for the _____ industry? How did you choose that area of specialty?
- Paul tells me that you are considering introducing a new (product/service) next year? How is that going?
- When I was looking at your website, I noticed _____. Can you tell me more about that?
- In reading the sales report, I noticed that you have steadily increased your use of Product A. What do you use Product A for predominantly?
- Your use of Product B has decreased over the years. Why is that?
- Paul told me about a shipping problem that occurred between our two companies several years ago. I know it was addressed and fixed. Have you experienced any shipping problems recently?
- Does our shipping process meet your standards?
- What are your goals for the coming year?
- Which one is your top priority?
- How can our company help with achieving those goals?
- Who are some of your favorite sales representatives?
- How do they help you and your business?
- At some point, would someone from your company be able to give me a tour of your facilities?

In most cases, I recommend that new hires go prepared with 10–12 questions that help them bond with and learn more about their new account. Most of the questions should be positive in nature, but they can certainly ask one or two that might involve a more serious discussion. The salespeople need to establish that they are there to work, not just "touch base" and a list of intelligent, thoughtful questions help achieve that goal.

A SALES PITCH

Salespeople make presentations. Salespeople sell. Clients expect it. To have the call come to a conclusion without the salesperson making a sales presentation has an incomplete feel to it. Together with the new hire, strategize about that first meeting.

When working with clients, I recommend the following as potential vehicles for presentations to larger accounts:

- New product or service
- Upgrades or enhancements to current product line
- Changes in service policies
- Discussion of lesser-known products or services

If your organization has plans to introduce a new product or announce major policy changes, let the new salesperson make the presentation. Sometimes nothing of tremendous importance is in the offing. In cases like these, don't force the new hire to make a presentation that wastes your valuable client's time.

Instead, create a sales event for the new hire. These could include:

- Year end special
- Purchase incentive
- Trial offer

Be imaginative. Look at the mix of products the client buys and come up with some sort of a "package purchase." Encourage the client to consider a new product or service by offering it on a trial basis or at no charge for a month. Motivate them to increase the volume of business they do with your company with a gift certificate or year-end rebate of some kind. When the benefits are made clear, most customers really enjoy these types of programs.

Many of the company presidents I work with resist this plan.

They tell me things like, "There are no major problems with that account. I don't need to create a special deal," or "I have my own profit margins to consider and they are tough price negotiators as it is," or "That account has been with us since my parents started the company 40 years ago. They aren't going anywhere."

The account may not be in jeopardy or have any outstanding problems. I'm not trying to create a drama where none exists. Rather, I'm encouraging you to think about the bigger picture. You and the new sales representative call on the largest account together and all you do is introduce the new rep. No selling of any kind goes on. If the sales representative visits this account every six weeks, he or she has to wait for that length of time before scheduling another call.

It probably took you a month or more to hire a new sales representative. The new rep then spent three weeks in the office receiving training. By the time the rep calls on them for the second time, the client really hasn't been sold to in roughly a business quarter or more.

Sobering, no? My plan encourages you to present your new salesperson as a trained and prepared professional who will show up and *sell* to the client right from the beginning. Some margin may indeed be sacrificed creating an interesting incentive or year-end rebate. Some time out of your day may be spent in coming up with an interesting trial offer. But it's in your best financial interest to organize a program for your best accounts and your new sales representative.

If nothing else motivates you, consider the reality of losing this valued customer. Isn't the time and trouble involved in getting the new hire off to a strong start worth the effort? Putting a plan in place will yield positive dividends for your company and the new hire.

10

Providing Sales Skills Training

Jake, the president of a stationery company, interviewed a salesperson with an impressive resume. She produced documentation to back up the noteworthy accomplishments. References she provided reinforced what she said about herself during the interview process. Jake happily offered her the open sales position.

Everything started out just fine. A born cold caller, this salesperson convinced prospect after prospect to commit to meetings and product presentations. After the presentations, however, most prospects remained in the pipeline months after Jake felt the deals should have been closed. She offered strong justifications for the lingering deals, but Jake remained unconvinced. He grew so frustrated with the excuses that he stopped meeting with her on a regular basis. He was afraid he'd lose his temper.

By pure coincidence, he found himself seated next to a former colleague of hers at an industry gathering. When the colleague asked about the salesperson, Jake heard himself giving a noncommittal answer. She proceeded to tell Jake that everyone at her company really liked this individual and wanted her to succeed. But the sales manager had to go with her to close almost all of her deals. After a while, the sales manager decided to put her on warning. She just couldn't close her own sales.

A stunned Jake tried to remain attentive and polite while speaking to his former colleague, but his thoughts were elsewhere. Mystery solved. The new sales representative has trouble closing. Her impressive sales numbers with her former employer were a result of the sales manager's efforts. How could he have known? What can he do about it now?

WITH THE EXCEPTION OF SUPERSTARS WHO ARE FEW AND FAR BETWEEN, most sales representatives, even those with years of experience, do not have *all* the skills and training they need to excel in *every* area of the sales cycle. Some might struggle, for instance, with getting past gatekeepers while others ask weak qualifying questions.

The great majority of salespeople, regardless of tenure, need sales training courses and supplementary training throughout their careers.

Large companies have candidates take a battery of pre-employment assessments to determine whether they are right for sales before continuing with the interview process. Through the assessment results they gain an understanding of their new employee's sales strengths and weaknesses. The new hire's sales manager will undoubtedly address any sales skills issues as they begin to work together.

In addition to a comprehensive new hire orientation, most large companies offer additional sales training in one form or another throughout the salesperson's career. They recognize that sales representatives who don't continue to upgrade their skills from time to time are prone to burnout or become complacent. They consider training and development to be an investment in their sales personnel.

Many smaller companies bypass the idea of pre-employment assessments and sales training altogether. Though tighter budgets play a role, I think money makes up just one part of the picture. Most salespeople in smaller companies are managed by someone without a formal sales background. The absence of assessments and sales training stems from a lack of understanding on this person's part about the traits of successful salespeople and what they need in the way of training and development throughout their careers.

Jake's painful story underscores my point. His all-too common experience speaks to what he *did not* do versus what he did do. Jake set up a formal interview process. He verified the claims on the salesperson's resume and checked her references. Strong cold calling efforts on the salesperson's part did help bring in a number of new customers for her former employer. The salesperson in question just didn't close those sales herself.

Had Jake assessed this salesperson before hiring her, he would have gotten the full picture of her sales abilities, poor closing skills, and all. During the interview process he could have asked specific questions about her approach to closing a sale.

More than that, the assessment would have told him exactly how poor her closing skills were. She might not have been capable of ever learning this critical skill.

If Jake had wanted to move ahead with hiring her, he could have provided the training necessary to address her problematic areas. He wouldn't have been clueless about this salesperson. Accurate information about her poor closing skills combined with the targeted training, *might* have changed the entire picture of her performance to date with his company.

HISTORY OF SALES TRAINING AND ASSESSMENTS

Prior to the 1900s salesmen functioned as independent businessmen who traditionally received their compensation as a percentage of or commissions on goods sold. Gradually, selling became less the realm of the entrepreneur and more another function of a corporation. This affected the salesmen's compensation. In many cases, their income changed from commission to a salary plus bonus.

As sales became a more formalized department in a large company, sales training came into existence. Many salesmen found themselves taking courses in salesmanship and reading literature on the psychology of selling. Some companies hired sales training specialists or retained such outside counsel as the Psychological

Psychological Corporation was started in 1921 by psychologist James McKeen Cattell. He was the president of the American Psychological Association and founder of Scientific Monthly.

Corporation to train and guide their salesmen.

Sales assessments have an interesting history as well. For many years, only large companies could afford to use them. These companies had the luxury of being able to interview people well in advance of needing to fill open positions. After asking the applicant to take the assessment, they were able to wait weeks for an industrial psychologist to interpret the results. The process was extensive and costly.

Today, greater awareness exists as to the importance of sales training and assessments. Both are available at a variety of price points. As a consequence, no business of any size has to avoid using these powerful tools to evaluate or educate their sales applicants or sales staff.

THE SALES PERSONALITY

Talkative. Glib. Persuasive. Outgoing. Friendly. When people think of the attributes that best describe salespeople some of these words come to mind. Men and women with those traits are told, often from a very young age, that they should definitely go into sales.

Hiring managers take an affable demeanor as a sign that a candidate is a natural for a sales position. Many assume that once they learn the product line, they will have little trouble succeeding. They think to themselves, "Customers will love meeting this person."

This stereotypical thinking about sales representatives causes problems during the hiring process. One of the most important character traits in determining whether someone will be successful in sales is money motivation. Money-motivated people have all kinds of personalities. Some are outgoing, some are shy, and others still are somewhere in the middle. Not every successful salesperson is outgoing and not every friendly person will succeed in sales.

Given the average president's tendency to select friendly and outgoing individuals for their open sales positions, I insist that my clients use some sort of pre-employment sales assessment as part of the hiring process. Learning from an unbiased assessment that their affable applicant has some real deficiencies as a salesperson helps most company presidents make a more informed hiring decision.

Different schools of thought exist as to when to use this tool. Some hiring managers assess candidates before meeting them. Others wait until after the telephone interview (if that's part of the process) or after the final candidates have been selected. I suggest that my clients assess as early in the process as possible to avoid getting attached to an engaging but unqualified candidate.

THE ASSESSMENTS

The experience of reading the assessment results for the first time shocks some company presidents. Candidates with stellar resumes might receive average to poor assessment scores. Those with more modest accomplishments may have far more impressive marks. Some presidents, on seeing that a candidate performed poorly on the assessment, swear they know best. They continue with the interviewing process and sometimes even hire these candidates.

Regardless of what the assessment tells you and how you choose to use the results, awareness of the candidate's strengths and weaknesses gives you a tremendous advantage over using information provided in their resume alone. As well, a competent assessment provides the type of data that's highly unlikely to come to light from a reference.

As an example, let's say you've asked applicants for your open sales position to take a sales assessment before you meet with them. The results for Candidate A are shown in figure 10-1.

The interpretation of these results: Weak prospector, strong qualifier, effective at handling objections, and competent closer.

As a hiring sales manager, the assessment results tell me that candidates with this profile experience difficulties when prospecting. When they make contact with a prospect they ask effective

Figure 10-1. Assessment Results for Candidate A

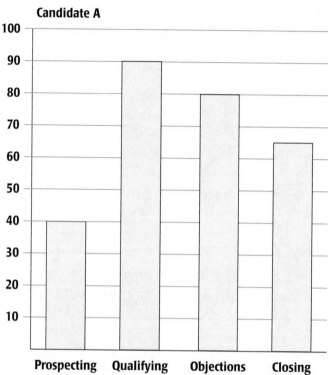

qualifying questions and handle objections well. Because they ask good questions and deal with the prospect's potential reservations, their pipeline has well-qualified candidates. Candidates like this aren't afraid to close. Their weak prospecting skills limit the number of qualified candidates available to close.

I would be interested in candidates with this profile, but I would have serious concerns about their prospecting skills. During the interview, I want several of my interview questions to focus on this issue. I might ask questions such as:

- On a scale from 1 to 10, how effective do you think you are at prospecting?
- Tell me about your prospecting methodology.
- What would a successful prospecting session look like for you in terms of numbers of calls/number of conversations?

- When speaking to a gatekeeper or receptionist who won't let you speak to a decision-maker, what's your strategy?
- The assessment gave you lower scores on prospecting. What are your thoughts on that?

Depending on how the questions are answered, I should come away with an understanding of how these candidates view their prospecting abilities. That combined with how much training I think they will need to become proficient at prospecting will influence my hiring decision.

The results for candidate B are as follows:

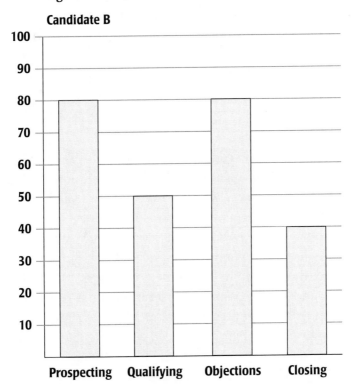

Figure 10-2. Assessment Results for Candidate B

The interpretation: Strong prospector and objection handler, average qualifier, and below average closer.

As the hiring manager, I am slightly less interested in candidates with this profile. Though more skilled at prospecting than the first candidate, once they make contact with the prospect they don't ask a lot of strong qualifying questions. This, combined with the their weak closing skills, tells me that they are afraid of asking tough questions or coming right out and asking for the sale.

Were I to interview candidates with traits like these, my questions around their qualifying and closing skills might look something like:

- What type of questions do you ask potential customers to determine whether they are a good fit for your product or service?
- If a prospect doesn't appear to be a strong match for your product, how do you handle the conversation?
- How do you gauge whether a prospect might be ready to buy?
- Give me an example of what you might say when closing a sale.
- On a scale of 1 to 10, how effective do you think you are at closing sales?
- The assessment gave you lower scores on closing. What are your thoughts on that?

In all likelihood, the candidate's answers to the questions will jibe with the findings in the assessment. Candidates with weak closing scores may give a weak answer when asked about their own closing technique. If they claim proficiency in certain skill areas and their responses and the assessment say otherwise, think seriously about passing on these applicants.

Between the candidate's resume, references, the face-to-face interviews, and the assessment, you now have a full look at this person as an employee and salesperson. Many presidents have told me that the first time they introduced assessments into the hiring process they felt very uncomfortable. They went on to say that once they hired the individual, though, they felt that they really knew whom they had brought into their organization and found this to be empowering.

SALES TRAINING

So you've hired a new sales representative. The assessment results and their responses during the interview process have left you feeling confident that the person needs a little help with prospecting for new business. Act on that feeling. Address this problem. The new rep's prospecting issues will not magically go away. Offer the person the opportunity to bolster those cold calling skills and both you and the new hire will realize greater sales revenue.

> **New hire orientation, no matter how meticulously planned, will focus on company and product knowledge, not sales skills.**

Start contacting sales training companies before the new hire's first day on the job. Learn about the various organizations and methodologies. Get recommendations from peers. Understand the costs. When speaking with these companies ask them how they would address a participant's pre-existing sales weaknesses. Choose a provider whose syllabus covers the areas your new hire needs help in.

Regardless of which training organization you select, be involved in this whole process. It takes so little time. Speak openly with the instructors about candidates' strengths and weaknesses before sending them to the first class. If the new hires attend class on Tuesday evenings, for instance, wish them good luck on Tuesday afternoon. On Wednesday or Thursday of that same week, discuss the class with the new hire. Ask questions such as:

- What did you talk about Tuesday night?
- What was the most important concept that you learned?
- How are you going to apply that day-to-day?
- What has changed for you since starting this training?

Your expression of interest will reinforce the fact that you're supportive of the salesperson. Be open-minded, as well. If there has been little or no formal sales training in your organization, the salesperson may be learning about new concepts and ideas that are not in step with how your company has operated in the past.

Accept this and be willing to consider making some changes to business procedures, even if they feel uncomfortable at first. To begin a discussion of this nature, ask questions like these:

- Is there anything I or someone else here can do to support you in using that new idea?
- Are we doing anything here at Company XYZ that's counter to what you're learning in class?
- Have you learned anything that you think the whole company might benefit from?

Lastly, once the salesperson has attended several sessions, pick up the phone and speak to his or her instructor. Confirm that the salesperson has been in attendance. Ask the instructors how they feel about the salesperson's progress. Protect your investment in the training and in this salesperson. When you've hired the right person, you'll find out that this individual is attending class, completing homework assignments, participating in the exercises and generally enjoying the experience.

Occasionally, a manager will be surprised to find out that the sales representative has skipped a few classes or shows up and is simply going through the motions. If this is the case, find out early in the process, discuss the situation with the salesperson, and take appropriate action. Don't wait until the training ends.

ORGANIZATIONAL FIT

If you as a manager have several sales representatives on staff and are hiring a new salesperson using the methodology I recommend in this book, you may be apprehensive about the cultural difference between your previous hires and your new employee. It's a valid concern.

My advice would be to assess the current sales staff for their strengths and weaknesses. If possible, sign them up for the same training that the new hire will be attending. In this way, you'll be strengthening the entire group's sales skills, creating a more homogeneous environment, and building a stronger sales culture.

When salespeople embrace training, it can significantly enhance their earning potential, as well as loyalty to the company. Avoid "hoping for the best" if the new hire struggles with certain aspects of selling. Instead, acknowledge the new hire's imperfections and help him or her become a better salesperson.

Salespeople appreciate and tend to have longer tenures with an employer who invests in their careers by providing supplementary or ongoing sales training.

11

Tracking Progress and Performance

Yvonne dislikes recording the results of each outgoing sales call she makes. Why does she need to go to the trouble every time anyway? Besides, sometimes she just leaves (another) message or hangs up after hearing the prospect's voicemail. Logging the specific type of call involves two extra steps that she doesn't have time for. Begrudgingly, she types l/m (left message) in the notes section (where she knows she isn't supposed to put it) and leaves yet another voice mail message for a prospect she's been trying to reach.

Maddening—there's no other word for it—maddening!! She's stayed late, skipped lunch, and come in early trying to have a conversation with this prospect, and she just can't get the person on the phone. She wishes Barbara, her manager and company president, knew how hard she's been working on trying to have a conversation with this guy.

Yvonne tries to reach another customer who told her to call at 1 pm, but the person doesn't answer. She writes 1:30 pm and the prospect's name on a piece of paper and sticks it on her computer screen. She'll grab lunch and try again in half an hour.

Barbara thinks Yvonne might have the potential to be a strong producer. Her independent nature and the way she chafes at any task that hints of conformity make her difficult to manage, though. Despite speaking to her about it on several occasions, Yvonne fails to record sales information in the software program with any consistency.

This causes Barbara difficulties when trying to coach Yvonne. She suspects that after an unproductive call or two, Yvonne gets discouraged and does something else for a while. Sales reports confirm that there are long stretches of time between her calls, as opposed to a one- or two-hour block of steady calling activity. Yvonne claims she does make calls for an hour or two and shows Barbara the notes section for each account to prove it.

Barbara finds the whole notes section discussion tedious and annoying. She doesn't have the time to scroll down the page and decipher all of Yvonne's notes. Logging a call correctly takes 10–15 seconds and the information provided is invaluable to her as a manager. Yvonne knows this. Although Barbara hired her, she feels she isn't doing a good job of helping her develop as a salesperson. She's unsure whether Yvonne will be successful with the company.

YVONNE DOES WORK HARD AND COULD VERY WELL SUCCEED AT HER NEW company. She absolutely never gives up when trying to reach a potential customer. She asks good questions and clearly knows when to stop wasting her time with someone who will never buy. Barbara's observation about her being a bit scattered is on the mark. She jumps around from task to task and could use some guidance in that area. Her attitude toward the software program will make forward progress difficult for both parties.

In this day and age, sales representatives must understand and use whatever sales software system their company selects. Other departments need the data a sales representative logs into the system to help them better understand the market and make critical decisions. Managers depend on the information to track sales performance and create sales reports.

What you expect from the salesperson, from a technology compliance standpoint, must be made clear in advance of the person coming to work for you.

Regardless of which software package your company uses, I would like to review the basic *types* of reports that I recommend anyone managing salespeople make a part of their sales information system. The look of these reports may differ from company to company. That's fine. I want to show the sort of data that I think should be included in the suite of sales reports that you use.

A group of strong sales reports should include:

- Daily call
- Productivity
- Pipeline
- Sales forecast
- Long-range sales forecast

THE DAILY CALL REPORT

Knowing how many calls your sales representatives make during a given day, as well as whom they are calling, is essential for those managing salespeople. Accounts are not all created equal. Some need to be called on more frequently than others. For example, one account may need a visit once a quarter while another needs a visit every six weeks. After establishing the call frequency for all of the salespeople's accounts, the data from this report confirms whether they are adhering to the schedule.

Some salespeople focus their efforts almost exclusively on new business. In this case, measurement centers on whether they are penetrating their territories. Are they visiting all the major accounts? How many prospecting calls are they making? Are they making sales calls throughout the entire territory?

A daily call report might look something like Figure 11-1.

Little additional information, such as how a call went or what the next step is, can be found in this report. Other reports show that level of detail. This report tells you how many calls the individual salespeople on your staff made, what type of call it was, whom they spoke to, and how long the call lasted. After taking a look at it, you should have a good idea of how reps spent some of their time that day with regard to sales/customer activity.

Figure 11-1. Daily Call Report

Sales Representative: Yvonne

Company	Contact	Date	Call Start	Call End	Call Type	Frequency
ABC Corporation	Sam	3/12/2010	8:32 am	8:57 am	PC	
123 Company	Jill	3/12/2010	9:20 am	9:21 am	F/U	4 wk
456 Organization	Martin	3/12/2010	10:00 am	10:35 am	PD	2 wk
EFG Associates	Lily	3/12/2010	11:00 am	11:01 am	PC	
789 Partners	George	3/12/2010	11:30 am	11:46 am	PC	
HIJ Company	Adrian	3/12/2010	1:00 pm	2:30 pm	A	6 wk
101 Company	Jeremy	3/12/2010	3:00 pm	3:05 pm	C/B	4 wk
KLM Corporation	Barbara	3/12/2010	3:32 pm	4:07 pm	C	8 wk
134 Associates	Cliff	3/12/2010	4:10 pm	4:17 pm	F/U	2 wk

Legend: PC = Prospecting Call, C = Conversation, F/U - Follow-up Call, C/B = Call Back, PD = Product Demonstration, A = In-Person Appointment

What to Look For
- Number of calls made in a row
- Specific types of calls
- Absence of certain types of calls
- Excessive numbers of certain types of calls
- Average length of call time

Questions to Ask
- How long are the gaps between calls?
- During the gaps, what was the rep doing?
- What tasks does the rep deal with in between calls?
- Why are there so many/so few of a particular type of call?

Observations
The salesperson featured in the above report makes a wide variety of calls (prospecting and follow-up) and speaks to the different types of accounts in his or her territory. However, the rep's calls are random and there are significant gaps between them.

For example, this salesperson completes the first call of the morning by 8:57 am and doesn't make another call for 20 minutes.

The third call of the day to the 456 Organization takes place 40 minutes after the second call. By 10:35 am only three calls are logged in. Though the rep does make prospecting calls, they are scattered throughout the day, instead of being made in one dedicated time block. No call of any kind takes place after 4:17 pm.

This may be an atypical day for this salesperson. It may not. Possibly the rep achieves his or her sales goals by fitting in a prospecting call here and there. More than likely, this stop and start pattern makes it more difficult for this sales rep to meet quota. To see patterns emerge, look at a week or a month's worth of calls rather than a single day.

Even being aware that a pattern exists can be challenging without this basic but very valuable information. Once you take a look at 20 or so of these daily call reports, you'll know your sales reps' habits well. With this information in hand, you can guide them in the areas you feel need improvement and let them know how pleased you are with their efforts in other areas.

THE PRODUCTIVITY REPORT

Those managing salespeople need a reasonably accurate summary of how many and which type of calls they make. The data often includes the number of outbound calls, conversations, voice mails, e-mails, customer meetings, product demonstrations, and proposals generated in a given day, week, or month. The report compares actual results against the benchmarks established for each activity.

Whether a sales staff exceeds or fails to meet the established productivity standards, the productivity report keeps the manager informed. When a salesperson or sales staff does struggle, looking at the raw numbers can offer insight into the problem(s).

Like the daily call report, the productivity report is simple and straightforward (Figure 11-2).

What to Look For
- Activities below quota
- Activities exceeding quota
- Consistently exceeding/failing to exceed in particular categories

Figure 11-2, Productivity Report

Weekly Production Report				
	Quota	**Actual**	**+/−**	**%**
PC	125	136	11	109%
C	10	8	(2)	80%
A	4	3	(1)	75%
PD	3	4	1	133%
PRO	2	2	0	100%

Legend: PC = Prospecting Call, C = Conversation with Decision Maker, A = In-Person Appointment, PD = Product Demonstration PRO = Proposal

Questions to Ask

- At which point in the sales cycle is the rep below/above productivity quota?
- In which areas is the rep consistently behind/ahead?
- Where the rep is below/above the productivity quota, how does it affect the next phase of the sales cycle?

Observations

After reviewing several of these reports, you should start to get an idea of where a sales representative might be having problems. Based strictly on the number of dial-outs, this particular representative seems to have no fear of prospecting. Convincing decision-makers to stay on the phone and have a conversation proves to be more difficult. Why? How does the rep's introduction sound? Is it brief yet persuasive? As a consequence of not speaking with enough decision-makers, this person often comes up short in the number of required appointments.

However, if they do meet with the sales representative, the decision-maker almost always gives the go-ahead to set a date for a product demonstration. Throughout this product demonstration, the salesperson must be saying and doing the right things because afterward most decision-makers request a proposal.

Salespeople with statistics like this show real potential. If they are willing to participate in sales training or be coached in the area of cold calling, their performance could be greatly improved. Understanding where they need additional help would be far more challenging without the productivity information.

Depending on the product and the length of the sales cycle, you may want to see these numbers daily. For others, a weekly or monthly report would suffice. Create the report and review it consistently. The straightforward and objective nature of this information makes for a great starting point from which to begin guiding the sales representatives. Anyone managing salespeople should have these numbers available to them.

THE PIPELINE

A sales cycle represents the approximate length of time and typical sequence of steps involved in bringing a sale to its conclusion. Do some sales take longer than others? Sure. Are some steps in the sales cycle more complicated than others? Of course. Can a salesperson occasionally skip a step altogether or get stuck at one step for what seems like forever? Yes and yes. Most sales follow a fairly consistent pattern, though.

During their work week, sales representatives call on prospects that are at different points in the sales cycle. They don't spend all day Tuesday making cold calls while devoting all day Wednesday to closing deals. The sales effort doesn't work that way. At 10 am the salesperson might be introducing herself to a prospect and at 11am conducting a webinar for another company. Later in the afternoon, she'll find herself answering a prospect's questions about her pricing proposal.

Good salespeople manage their pipeline, which means that they work with many prospects concurrently.

The pipeline report consists of all those prospects being actively pursued by a sales representative and separates them by their appropriate phase in the sales cycle. This information allows you to keep track of the total number of prospects the salesperson is working with at any given point. You can tell how quickly a prospect progresses from one stage to the next or be aware when a prospect drops out altogether.

Here are examples of typical pipeline phases:

- Phase I. Decision-maker expresses interest in product or service
- Phase II. Salesperson meets with decision maker
- Phase III. Decision-maker participates in product demonstration
- Phase IV. Proposal submitted
- Phase V. Sale closed/sale lost

It helps if you and the sales reps agree on these phases. You will experience greater buy-in on their part. Naming the phases adds consistency, as well. When anyone on the sales staff refers to a prospect being in Phase 3, or the "demo complete" phase, everyone will know that the salesperson has completed a product demonstration and that the decision maker was present. This holds true for the rest of the company, as well. When marketing or finance understands what each phase means, you are starting to see the development of a sales culture.

New salespeople have the most to gain, though. Understanding the sales cycle early on and being able to differentiate among the phases in the sales process will help them avoid the bloated pipeline and long, unproductive sale cycles that sometimes undermine a new hires.

A pipeline report looks something like shown in Figure 11-3 (pages 151 to 155).

What to Look For

- Number of prospects in each phase
- Number of prospects stuck in one phase for a long time
- Number of prospects dropping out altogether in a particular phase

Questions to Ask

- What is the average time a prospect spends in each phase?
- Why are there so few/so many prospects in a particular phase?

Figure 11- 3. Pipeline Report

Phase I								
Company	**Decision Maker**	**Prod A**	**Prod B**	**Est Buy**	**Est Sale Prod A**	**Est Sale Prod B**	**Next Step/Mfg**	
A Corporation	Maura	X		Q2			Meet with decision maker	
B Corporation	Jack		X	Q1			Difficulty scheduling mtg	
C Corporation	Doris		X	Q2			Call admin asst	
D Corporation	Peter		X	Q3			Speak with IT	
E Corporation	Raymond	X	X	Q2			Meet with decision maker	
F Corporation	Dudley			Q1			Call dir of mktg	
G Corporation	Maurice	X		Q3			Meet with decision maker	

- During which phase do most prospects drop out?

Observations

Just like the two preceding reports, the pipeline teems with great information about this sales representative and shows you where you might want to get involved. Before I discuss that, however, I want to make a comment about the Next Step/Meeting section. Some may see that section as too brief to get enough information, and I would agree. The real detail can and should be found wherever your software program has a designated area for lengthier descriptions or notes. If you're concerned about a particular account, you should be able to find detailed descriptions in this area.

As a manager reviewing this report, I see that the sales representative has a full pipeline with the requisite number of prospects in each phase. I want to recognize this person for that effort. I also notice that a number of the prospects get stuck in one phase or another. Let's look at Phase I B Corporation. The prospect won't schedule a follow-up meeting. Does the sales representative fail to schedule the next meeting during the current one? If a prospect makes getting together again difficult, does the rep ask why? These

Figure 11-3. Pipeline Report (continued)

Phase II											
Company	Decision Maker	Prod A	Prod B	Est Buy	Est Sale Prod A	Prob %	Est Prod A	Est Sale Prod B	Prob %	Est Prod B	Next Step/Mfg
H Corporation	Tom		X	Q1				$17,000	60%	$10,200	Product Demo 2/19
I Corporation	James	X		Q2	$39,000	80%	$31,200				Schedule 2nd Mtg
J Corporation	Martha	X	X	Q2	$56,000	502%	$28,000				Product Demo 3/1
K Corporation	Zachary	X	X	Q1	$12,000	502%	$6,000	$29,000	50%	$14,500	Meet to choose between prods
L Corporation	Jill		X	Q1				$19,000	90%	$17,100	Won't return calls
M Corporation	Adam	X		Q2	$25,000	70%	$17,500				Product Demo 2/25
Total					$132,000		$82,700	$65,000		$41,800	

Figure 11-3. Pipeline Report (continued)

Phase III											
Company	Decision Maker	Prod A	Prod B	Est Buy	Est Sale Prod A	Prob %	Est Prod A	Est Sale Prod B	Prob %	Est Prod B	Next Step/Mfg
N Corporation	Christine	X		Q2	$62,000	90%	$55,800				Give 2nd Product Demo, Operations
O Corporation	Jeff	X		Q2	$31,000	50%	$15,500				Meet re: Pricing
P Corporation	Gary	X		Q1	$19,000	80%	$15,200				Submit Proposal
Q Corporation	Barbara		X	Q1				$48,000	70%	$33,600	Bring IT to talk to their IT Dept
R Corporation	Robert		X	Q1				$32,000	80%	$25,600	Submit Proposal
S Corporation	George	X		Q2	$29,000	80%	$23,200				2nd mtg with George
Total					$141,000		$109,700	$80,000		$59,200	

Figure 11-3. Pipeline Report (continued)

Phase IV											
Company	Decision Maker	Prod A	Prod B	Est Buy	Est Sale Prod A	Prob %	Est Prod A	Est Sale Prod B	Prob %	Est Prod B	Next Step/Mfg
T Corporation	Sam	X		Q1	$71,000	70%	$49,700				Proposal in Committee
U Corporation	Ari		X	Q2				$34,000	50%	$17,000	Propoal being signed
V Corporation	Ellen		X	Q2				$42,000	80%	$33,600	Propoal being signed
W Corporation	Frank	X		Q1	$18,000	90%	$16,200				Proposal stuck. B won't return calls
Total					$89,000		$65,900	$76,000		$50,600	

Figure 11-3. Pipeline Report (continued)

Phase V											
Company	Decision Maker	Prod A	Prod B	Est Buy	Est Sale Prod A	Prob %	Est Prod A	Est Sale Prod B	Prob %	Est Prod B	Next Step/Mfg
X Corporation	William	X		Q1	$59,000	100%	$59,000				Closed
Y Corporation	Tamara		X	Q2				$13,000	100%	$13,000	Closed
Z Corporation	Ryan	X		Q2	$33,000	100%	$33,000				Closed
Total					$92,000		$92,000	$76,000		$13,000	

questions need to be asked and the answers explored.

The L Corporation in Phase II has an issue, as well. The decision-maker met with the sales representative but has stopped returning the rep's calls. Why might that be happening? Based on the decision-maker's current behavior, why does the salesperson feel that the L Corporation has a 90% chance of closing? Could the salesperson be overly optimistic? There may be a plausible explanation for this, but as a sales manager I would like to have a conversation about the situation. Unreturned phone calls rarely mean good news in sales.

In Phase III I notice that the sales representative responsible for calling on the N Corporation is estimating that there is a 90% chance that the sale will close. I want to find out what this sales rep needs to do to close the sale. More importantly, I know this is one tough account and that this sale in particular has been problematic. I want to make sure the rep understands how proud I am that he or she was able to bring the sale to this point.

Continuing on to Phase IV, the W Corporation will not sign or return the proposal even though the decision-maker received it

Reports not only let you know what a sales representative is up to, they provide great opportunities to make positive comments on their performance, as well. You should always be looking for reasons to praise your sales representatives.

weeks ago. Here we have another example of the sales representative struggling with potential sales that are "stuck." A strong manager will brainstorm with the sales representative to come up with ways to get this proposal dislodged and signed.

All sales reports offer opportunities for you to applaud or criticize a salesperson's performance. The pipeline report highlights some of the plain hard work that goes into taking a sale from beginning to end like almost no other.

THE SALES FORECAST

The single most important document generated in most sales organizations, a sales forecast has multiple purposes including:

- Holding salespeople accountable for the deals they intend to close at the end of each month
- Determining which opportunities need executive attention
- Helping to estimate revenue
- Paving the way for post-sale product or service delivery

The accuracy of this report strongly affects the entire organization. Unfortunately, many people confuse the pipeline report with the sales forecast.

The pipeline report and the sales forecast both show prospects at different phases of the sales process. The difference lies in the fact that the sales forecast shows only those prospects in the final stages of *purchasing* the product or service.

The pipeline report enables you to track how many prospects agree to a product demonstration. You know that completing a certain number of product demonstrations will typically result in a percentage of decision-makers being interested in a proposal. Seeing a product demonstration by no means guarantees that that the prospect will buy the product. In fact, if the demonstration does not go well, or the decision-maker prefers another company's product, the sales representative will probably not close the deal.

For this reason, I recommend that my clients allow no prospect to appear on the forecast *until* the decision-maker has seen a product demonstration (or the equivalent in a service industry) and has expressed interest in moving to the next level. Though difficult advice to follow at first, most of my clients agree that using the product demonstration as a "gatekeeper" ultimately makes for a more realistic sales forecast report.

The sales forecast report shown below contains:

- Prospect names
- Sales opportunity sizes
- Product/service a customer seems most interested in purchasing
- Sales representative's best estimate of which sales will close during the next 30, 60, or 90 days

All of the sales revenue is totaled at the bottom and compared against the salesperson's quota. This gives you a strong indication of whether a salesperson will achieve his or her sales goal for the given time period. In most companies, the Sales Forecast Report is due at the beginning of each month. Some presidents ask for a mid-month revision (Figure 11-4).

Most sales reports teem with great information and sometimes serve to warn a president about potential problems. The potential sales shown on the sales forecast might be a cause for celebration or function as a shrill alarm. The accuracy of the information provided determines sales revenue for the month or quarter. Failure to bring in enough sales revenue over a period of time leads to staff reductions, cash flow issues, and most drastically—companies going out of business.

Figure 11-4. Sales Forecast

January		
Company	**Product A**	**Product B**
Company ABC	$24,000	
Comany DDD		$28,000
Company EEE	$76,000	
Company BBB	$47,000	
Total	$147,000	$28,000
February		
Company FFF		$10,000
Comany GGG	$52,000	
Company HHH	$25,000	
Company III		
Company JJJ		$16,000
Company LLL	$39,000	
Total	$116,000	$26,000
March		
Company MMM	$58,000	
Company NNN		$11,000
Company OOO	$21,000	
Company QQQ	$13,000	
Company RRR		$19,000
Total	$92,000	$30,000

Figure 11-4. Sales Forecast (continued)

Product A

	January	February	March	Total
Total	$147,000	$116,000	$92,000	$355,000
Quota	$100,000	$100,000	$100,000	$300,000
Differences	$47,000	$18,000	($8,000)	$55,000

Product B

Total	$28,000	$26,000	$30,000	$84,000
Quota	$25,000	$25,000	$25,000	$75,000
Differences	$3,000	$1,000	$5,000	$9,000

What to Look For

- Percentage of months at or above quota
- Number of accounts in each month
- Amount of revenue for each prospect
- Sales of different products

What to Ask

- In which months (1, 2, or 3) is the rep typically above or below quota?
- Does revenue usually drop in any one month in particular?
- How many accounts drop out/get added from one month to the next?
- Does the rep have an easier/more difficult time achieving quota in one product line vs. another?

Observations

In January and February, the sales representative stands at $47,000 and $16,000 ahead of their quota, respectively. By March, the rep misses quota by $8,000. As the rep gets closer and closer to the month in which he or she is supposed to close the business, the revenue decreases significantly. Why? Does the rep have a tendency to overestimate a prospect's interest in the beginning of the sales cycle? What is this person's overall performance against quota for the year? Do they miss quota frequently?

While further examining the sales forecast, I notice an inconsistency between the two product lines. This salesperson more accurately predicts the sales revenue they'll bring in for Product B while struggling to do the same with Product A. Consistently achieving quota for Product B appears to be a little easier. Why? Does the rep say or do anything differently when prospecting or conducting product demonstrations? Can he or she articulate what that might be?

Anyone managing the sales rep would certainly be curious and start asking questions. None of these observations would be possible without a thorough and accurate Sales Forecast Report to review for several months running.

The stylistic presentation and theory behind the Sales Forecast differs from company to company and president to president. One school of thought says the total revenue shown in the forecast should be two to three times the amount needed to achieve quota. Others feel that only those deals that are highly likely to close in a given month or quarter should be on the forecast. Some prefer a probability forecast (the amount of the sale multiplied by the percentage chance that it will close that month).

When in sales manager mode, I choose the second style mentioned. Sales representatives should include only those deals that they feel will have a strong probability of closing in the stated period. By following this line of reasoning, they fully commit to finalizing those deals in the time frame promised. Any other sales forecast, to me, is a glorified pipeline. Not everyone will agree.

Sales forecasts are dynamic documents created for and used by the entire sales organization. The best forecasts increase sales force effectiveness. When the information contained within the report benefits a multitude of other departments, you've created the right sales forecast for your organization.

THE LONG-RANGE SALES FORECAST

Often overlooked, long range forecasts have a place in the portfolio of reports for those managing salespeople. Prospects in this report have told the sales representative that they are budgeted for and are committed to purchasing a product or service at some point in the future. The reason for the delayed purchase usually involves an expiring contract or a large capital expenditure that needs to go through a formal budgeting or bid process.

Typically, the *long-range forecast* keeps track of prospects planning to buy anywhere from four months to two years from the time of the initial contact with the sales representative. (See Figure 11-5.)

Many of these long-range sales involve RFPs, intense competition, or the possible replacement of the prospect's current provider. Sales like these usually require executive involvement at some point. This report helps management prepare accordingly.

What to Look For
- Number of prospects in report
- Different industries represented
- Size of each potential sale

Questions to Ask
- How did the rep find out about these sales?
- Who are the main competitors in each case?
- What type of assistance does or will the rep need?
- Is the rep aware of almost all of the long-term potential sales in his or her territory?

Observations
Neither large nor complex, this report has little data to analyze. Top performing salespeople know about most of the prospective sales in their geographic area: those that will close quickly, those that might take some time, and those that will occur in the future. This report helps you confirm that the new hire has the capability to uncover and distinquish among the different types of sales.

Doing the nitty-gritty work involved in closing sales involves discipline and focus. Knowing potential sales exist in the foreseeable future provides a needed "lift" for the sales representative and his or her manager during some of the more difficult sales days.

Figure 11-5. Long Range Forecast

Company	Q4 Prod A	Q4 Prod B	Q1 20xx Prod A	Q1 20xx Prod B	Q2 20xx Prod A	Q2 20xx Prod B	Q3 20xx Prod A	Q3 20xx Prod B	Q4 20xx Prod A	Q4 20xx Prod B	Q1 20xx Prod A	Q1 20xx Prod B
Company A					$24,000							
Company B										$16,000		
Company C						$88,000						
Company D	$9,000											
Company E											$35,000	
Company F								$26,000				
Company G				$49,000								
Company H												
Totals	$9,000			$49,000	$24,000	$88,000		$26,000		$16,000	$35,000	

THE NEW HIRE

New hires listen carefully to what you tell them, but they pay even closer attention to what they actually observe their peers doing.

Salespeople are greatly influenced by the real-time behavior of the sales staff. If they can clearly see the other salespeople entering data into the software program and coming to sales meetings with the proper reports, they will understand the importance of sales reporting to their new organization. When new hires observe the sales staff being held accountable for the content and quality of their reports they will know that the same rules apply to them.

On the other hand, they may notice that only some of the sales representatives use the software program. Maybe the entire staff uses the program, but they go quickly through the motions of filling out their sales reports with little attention to detail. New hires will realize that they don't have to put in a lot of effort either. Once they do turn a report in, if they see that you either ignore it or glance at it every now and again, they will become indifferent to the process, just like the rest of the staff.

Help new hires learn about the reporting system in the early weeks of their tenure. If possible (and as long as it can be deleted afterward), have them enter some made-up information and then generate a few reports. Let them put in the data for another salesperson and then run that individual's reports.

Their ability to use the system correctly and consistently should play a big role in the overall evaluation process during their first three months. Set the expectation that their skills should improve every day. Ask them to demonstrate appropriate proficiency before a monthly review.

ADDITIONAL REPORTS

Companies rely on all kinds of reports. I mentioned five that I feel should form the cornerstone of a sales reporting system for sales organizations. Other reports of importance could include:

- Contract expiration
- Shipment of goods
- Gross profit
- Overstocks
- Shortages
- Production schedules

If a sales reporting system is brand new to your existing staff, introduce the reports I recommend one at a time. Make sure that the sales staff understands what information you're looking for, why it's important, and how it will help them increase sales. Be available to answer questions and offer assistance when they struggle to provide the right data.

Once the entire sales staff correctly completes a report and turns it in by the due date three times in a row, you can move on to the next one. The report has been successfully integrated into your sales culture.

12

Sponsor Motivating Sales Contests

As she schedules the appointment in the sales software system, Samantha can barely contain her excitement. She's set up two appointments with decision-makers this week. She feels a little dubious about the first appointment. Eager to start contributing to the sales effort, she feels like she pushed the prospect into seeing her. She won't be shocked if he cancels at some future point.

But this second appointment was the real deal for sure. The conversation they had about how her company's product might potentially help the decision-maker's business was encouraging. Samantha feels as if her presentation skills and product knowledge are coming together at last.

Really needing to share her good news, she tells the company president about her two appointments as he walks by her desk. "Oh...uh... great. Well, isn't that what we pay your for?" he says as he laughs nervously. Samantha feels foolish. "How stupid of me," she thinks to herself. "Two appointments. Big deal. No wonder he looked at me like I was an idiot!"

She feels deflated. The thrill of setting up those two meetings is gone. Samantha feels better after she calls her best friend. Knowing how nervous she has been about getting off to a good start at this company, the friend suggests meeting for dinner to celebrate. That sounds great to Samantha.

HAVING THEIR MANAGER RECOGNIZE EARLY PRE-SALES SUCCESSES, LIKE scheduling the first appointment or webinar, means a lot to new hires. They spend many weeks familiarizing themselves with the new product or service, getting to know their co-workers, learning the computer system, and even figuring out how the office coffeemaker works. Their early, tangible accomplishments are important to them.

Unfortunately, many business executives fail to help the new sales rep celebrate these beginning victories in a meaningful manner. They find it puzzling when new hires need praise or some sort of additional reward just for doing the job they were hired to do. Some business executives see it as neediness and it makes them uncomfortable.

Most of my clients understand that salespeople are motivated by the ability to earn either commissions or bonuses above and beyond their base salaries. Many think that the compensation plan alone should be enough incentive. After all, how many other employees even have the chance to earn a commission?

> **No matter how** motivating a compensation plan may be, presidents need to do more to ensure that their sales reps remain energized and inspired on a daily, weekly, monthly basis, not just quarterly or annually.

Sometimes clients find it difficult to comprehend that salespeople *expect* to be paid commissions or bonuses if they achieve quota. It comes with the territory and is one of the attractions of the profession. That's where sales contests come in. The possibility of a reward above and beyond a paycheck and bonus helps salespeople focus and stretch to reach for a goal that they might have thought unattainable.

Convincing most of my clients to sponsor contests for their sales staff has always been one of my biggest challenges. Some of them don't really understand sales contests. Others can picture only big-ticket prizes like expensive island vacations or giant home entertainment systems. They feel overwhelmed.

There are those who feel incensed that sales representatives would need anything more than the lucrative compensation plan to motivate them. They won't even discuss the subject. A client once said to me, "I don't have contests for shipping or accounts payable. Why all the hullabaloo over sales?"

Well, maybe shipping and accounts payable would enjoy a contest or two. I don't know. Those departments fall out of my area of expertise. I know sales and sales management. Even the most motivated salesperson needs and enjoys the occasional sales contest. If you are serious about running a sales organization, it's something that needs to be done.

In Walter A. Friedman's book *Birth of a Salesman: The Transformation of Selling in America* (Harvard University Press, 2005), he talks about how large, successful corporations in the early 20th century such as Burroughs, Equitable Insurance, NCR, and The American Multigraph Sales Company began to sponsor sales contests. He writes:

> Because the sales force worked offsite, managers could not directly oversee their work. In order to ensure that sellers remained motivated, they created various compensation schemes, and they also pursued other strategies designed to increase pressure, such as setting up contests like the "NCR Derby" or the Burroughs "Auto Rally."
>
> The American Multigraph Sales Company, for example, staged a mock war between the salesmen and an imagined "State of Depression." The war game, a three-month sales campaign, was launched with a special "War Extra" edition of the house newsletter. Bronze, silver, and gold crosses were given to those performing "Signal Sales Service." And those who sold less than a specified minimum ($500) were considered "wounded, crippled, sick, [or] exhausted" and sent to the "Base Hospital" for recovery.

Though some of these ideas may seem old-fashioned to us now, the basic premise of a sales contest remains the same: recognizing achievement above and beyond and offering prizes that the salespeople find motivating.

My father was a sales manager and I watched him and my mom take a number of company-sponsored trips to various places all over the world. He would talk to me in general terms about the sales revenue goals he and his staff had to achieve to win those trips. I understood from an early age that those trips weren't given to him. He and his salespeople had to earn them.

When I was in sales, I won a number of prizes from assorted sales contests and thoroughly enjoyed the process. I grew up in a sales household and became a salesperson myself. I worked for companies with national sales forces and just assumed that all companies ran sales contests. I thought all salespeople enjoyed contests as one of the perks of being in the profession.

NEGATIVE ATTITUDES

After I started my consulting practice and worked with a few clients, I was truly taken aback by how resistant they were to creating these contests. Once I saw the problem, I decided to have a conversation with several of them about their opposition to sponsoring one. I asked them to be candid and these are some of their statements:

- I feel silly handing a $50 gift certificate to an employee who has the potential to earn six figures. It seems ridiculous.
- Giving out an award feels very awkward. I know it should be exciting and I'm sort of reserved. I don't think I'm very good at it.
- During the interview process they went on and on about how self-motivated they were. If they are so self-motivated why do they need any of this?
- I resent all the catering I have to do for the salespeople. This is just one more thing.
- It feels like bribery.
- What if the salespeople are lying about some of their results? I don't want to be taken advantage of or look like a fool.
- It takes too much to administer these contests. I have a lot to do.

Though somewhat depressing, this was really good information for me to have. I could tell a few of my clients felt badly about revealing their true feelings. They knew what an unapologetic advocate I was for sales contests. But their honesty forced me to re-examine the way in which I approached my clients about the subject.

Just because I was excited about sales contests, understood their importance, and couldn't wait to create the first one didn't mean other business executives necessarily felt the same way, especially those who lacked a traditional sales background.

I realized that discussing sales contests was no different, in some ways, than talking to my clients about the importance of sales forecasts or performance reviews. All are part of sales force management. I've learned to tone down my enthusiasm and make the subject of sales contests a part of the ongoing, broad-based discussion. I don't downplay their importance, but I don't have an expectation that the business executive will be enthusiastic about them either.

Sometimes people get confused about the differences between sales bonuses, commissions, contests, and SPIFs. Let's clear that up.

A competition that rewards superior performance, **sales contests** can be short or long in duration. Salespeople receive prizes and/or additional compensation for achieving a goal over and above their regular quota. The payment is in addition to their salary and commission or bonus.

Typically paid out annually or quarterly, a **bonus** is a percentage of the salesperson's salary. With bonuses, the better the performance, the higher the percentage or gross amount of the payout.

Commission is a percentage of the value of the product or service sold.

Special Performance Incentive Funds (SPIFs) target specific products or services and pay a pre-determined amount or percentage for each one sold.

MONEY VS. GIFT CERTIFICATES

I have long been an advocate of gift certificates over a check or cash as a prize for winning a sales contest. Though appreciated, cash gets mixed up with the other money in a rep's wallet and gets used to pay for dry cleaning and groceries. A check gets deposited and goes toward paying for a child's braces or the mortgage.

Not so with gift certificates. Let's say a new rep wins a gift certificate to his or her favorite restaurant. The rep really can't use it for anything else. The salesperson will no doubt ask a friend or significant other to go along. This person will know where the gift certificate came from and help the rep celebrate. Dinner on the company is tangible proof of the rep's sales achievement.

LONG VS. SHORT

Some sales contests are very short and involve small amounts of money. A salesperson with the highest gross sales for the week might win a gift certificate to a favorite coffee shop. Others last much longer. Salespeople who exceed their annual quota by greater than 10% may end up on a beach in the Bahamas.

If sales contests have been virtually non-existent at your company, I would advise you to start with short, focused, and inexpensive challenges. These contests should be held at regular intervals and be tailored to the individual participants. Offer a modest dollar value ($150 or less), have clear rules, and make the contest brief (three months maximum).

It's also perfectly acceptable, especially in the case of the new hire, to have a few different contests running at the same time. Acknowledge different milestones and accomplishments. A motivated sales rep who feels recognized for doing a sometimes difficult job makes the creation of these contests well worth the effort.

Many types of gift certificates are available for short-term sales contests. Examples of great tangible prizes include gift certificates to favorite:

- Stores
- Restaurants
- Amusement Parks

Other prizes might include tickets to:

- Sporting Events
- Concerts

- Museums
- Movies

Other ideas might be:

- A dish filled with the winner's favorite candy
- Use of a parking space for a month
- A matching donation to a favorite charity
- Taking a valued colleague out to lunch on the company

For new hires, contests without time frames and sales revenue requirements work best. The completion of each contest will probably be achieved during different weeks so that the prizes are staggered. A group of contests like the ones below or something similar will keep them focused and motivated.

Here are some suggested goals and rewards for the new hire:

Figure 12-1. Suggested Contest Goals

Contest	Goal	Prize
Conversations w/ decision-makers	Complete 10	Gift Certificate to favorite restaurant
Meetings (phone or in-person w/decision-makers)	Complete 5	Movie tickets and $35 for babysitter
Product demos/ webinars for decision-makers	Complete 1	Four one-day passes to amusement park

Throughout this book I have talked about developing a sales culture within your organization. Creating a series of short, fun, winnable contests that reward new hires for their pre-sales efforts helps that culture begin to take shape.

IT'S NOT JUST MONEY

Some folks think that salespeople respond to one thing and one thing only—money. In terms of their overall outlook, I believe this to be true. But when it comes to rewards and recognition, my experience has been that they place a lot of value on genuine praise from their manager, non-sales executives, and their peers.

Examples of rewards that cost little or no money and have great motivational value are:

- Congratulatory calls from non-sales executives in the company
- Handwritten notes of congratulations
- A plaque or trophy
- Recognition at a staff meeting

Involve Others

Rewards like the four mentioned above require a little extra effort and thought as opposed to the relatively minor task of purchasing a gift certificate. As both a sales manager and a sales consultant, I often reach out to non-sales executives within an organization. I've asked them, for instance, to call salespeople to congratulate them on a particular accomplishment (it does not always have to be a closed sale). I have never had anyone turn me down.

Some seem surprised to be asked. Others want to fully understand what they are congratulating the sales rep for before they place the call (completely understandable). But they all do it and do it with enthusiasm. Some will tell me the phone isn't good enough and insist on congratulating the sales representative in person. The sales representative always seems thrilled to receive the call or visit. More than once the rep has run into my office to "share" the good news with me. I always feign surprise.

Handwritten Notes

Resist the urge to dash off a quick e-mail to recognize a new hire's accomplishment. Keep nice stationery on hand in your office. Take the time to come up with the right words that set the tone for what you want to say. Include a handwritten note of congratulations to accompany a gift certificate or acknowledge a new hire's milestone. Salespeople appreciate these gestures.

A lot of reps keep notes of this kind tacked to a bulletin board for all to see. Others are more private and save the notes in a desk drawer or separate file. When motivation is needed, I've seen many sales representatives look at or take them out and re-read them.

Plaques or Trophies

Recognizing certain accomplishments with a small trophy or plaque adds some fun. What if you gave your new hire a quota of three product demonstrations for the month and the new rep completed five—a company record. Giving the rep a plaque would be a meaningful acknowledgment of this accomplishment. Salespeople enjoy these gestures. The effort promotes good will and costs little.

Staff Meetings

Staff meetings offer a tremendous opportunity to acknowledge new hires (and tenured sales representatives, as well). It makes the meetings interesting and gives the other salespeople an opportunity to hear about what's going on with their new co-worker.

I never asked permission or gave any advance warning. I simply shared the new hire's recent victory or major accomplishment with the group. The other reps were always generous with applause and congratulations. They remembered what it was like to be the new kid, I'm sure.

Forward-thinking business executives prepare in advance. They make sure to have a few gift certificates or business stationery on hand "just in case." Handing a sales representative an impromptu prize or note for effort above and beyond provides great motivation.

Aᴅᴅɪᴛɪᴏɴᴀʟ Bᴇɴᴇꜰɪᴛs

There are other, less obvious benefits to running sales contests that a lot of executives don't often consider. Let's say that your new sales representative has a quota of three product demonstrations for the first month. In the rep's second month, the quota increases to six. From your discussions with the rep you know that he is feeling a bit intimidated about these additional demos.

> **Sales contests provide great and sometimes unexpected coaching opportunities.**

Create a contest that rewards the new rep with movie tickets, as an example, for completing seven demos in that second month, one more than the required six. By doing so you are helping reps see that they can indeed achieve even more than what is expected. Hopefully, with more time and experience, the rep will be able to exceed other goals that initially seem daunting.

As their manager, you might observe new hires struggling with a particular contest that you know they are motivated to win. Work with them to determine what might be going wrong. Ask them at which junctures of the sales cycle they feel they might be having trouble. Offer any support necessary to help them overcome the obstacle. Sales reps greatly appreciate a manager's efforts to help them win a contest.

PROVE OUT THE ROI

New sales representatives get caught up in a whirlwind of intense and diverse orientation activities. Sales contests can bring focus to their day and remind them of why they are there in the first place. As the orientation process winds down and they have won a few contests, you can begin to demonstrate how challenging themselves—with or without a contest—to exceed their goals will ultimately affect their paychecks.

Suppose that new hires working for your company will be expected to conduct 12 product demonstrations a month once they've completed their probationary period. Walk them through the financial benefits if they are able to conduct one additional product demonstration per month going forward (Figure 12-2).

Let's say that the average tenured sales representative in your organization has a ratio of 12-7-3. For every 12 product demonstrations they conduct they will most likely send out 7 proposals. Of those 7 proposals, 3 typically result in closed sales. If the sales representative were to conduct one extra product demonstration per month, the results might look that shown in Figure 12-3.

Figure 12-2. Minimum Productivity

	Product Demonstrations	Proposals	Closed Sales
Monthly Productivity	12	7	3
Annual Productivity	144	34	36

Figure 12-3. Increased Productivity

	Product Demonstrations	Proposals	Closed Sales
Monthly Productivity	13	8	3.5
Annual Productivity	156	96	42

Now the ratio has changed to 13-8-3.5. Increasing the number of completed product demonstrations boosts the number of proposals by 1, which boosts the number of closed sales by 0.5. Figure 12-4 shows what that could mean over the course of a year.

Figure 12-4. Increased Earnings

	Sales	Average Sale	Total Revenue	5% Commission
	42	$35,000	$1,470,000	$73,500
	36	$35,000	$1,260,000	$63,000
Difference	6	$35,000	$210,000	$10,500

Gift certificates are a lot of fun and handwritten notes are greatly appreciated, but over $10,000 in additional income—that's exciting and what sales is *all about*. With a tiered compensation plan, making six extra sales per year might even bump the sales rep into a higher commission bracket.

If new sales reps have exceeded their goals and been rewarded with some type of prize early on, they have proven to themselves that they can surpass expectations. That in itself makes a discussion about exceeding future objectives easier. Sales reps believing that they can increase their income through their own hard work is the most desired result of creating several interesting, fun, challenging, and rewarding sales contests.

Good salespeople like to compete, win, and be recognized for their efforts. By setting up a series of contests in which the new salesperson realizes success during their first few weeks and months with your organization, you're reinforcing the idea that you hire and reward winners. You want your new salesperson to be focused and to start gaining momentum as quickly as possible. Sales contests represent the perfect vehicle.

Part Three

Evaluating the New Hire

13

Conducting Performance Reviews: The 30-Day Review

Nervously, Rex begins to conduct an online product demonstration for the company president. They've worked together only twice since he started his new job, so he feels somewhat uncomfortable around her. She watches intently as he begins to discuss the image on the computer screen. He makes a mistake, loses his place, and then quickly gets back on track. The president asks three questions about pricing. Rex answers the first two easily but struggles on the third.

After the presentation, the president asks him to come into her office. She says, "Your product demo is good overall, but still needs a little work. It gets a bit long toward the middle. I've asked around and everyone seems to think you're doing a good job. It looks like this will work out. Let's talk again in a few weeks when your training period has ended."

Rex leaves her office feeling wary. He wonders whom the president spoke to and what they said about him. What did she mean when she said his product demo was long in the middle? Does she mean boring or just too long from a time standpoint? Overall, she doesn't seem displeased. He's relieved because he likes his new job.

He would have liked to brainstorm with her about an objection that came up during his last three sales calls. He doesn't think his response to the objection was particularly strong. But he worries that asking her about it would make him look weak. Well, maybe he should just be glad that his training period will probably end successfully. After his conversation with the president, he feels fairly confident he'll be offered a full-time sales position.

REX DOESN'T HAVE MUCH OF A RELATIONSHIP WITH THE PRESIDENT, HIS boss. They spend little time together and her abrupt manner causes him to feel inhibited about going to her for help. That's too bad because she's pleased with his performance overall. It's just that she's busy and he seems like he's doing OK, so she's leaving him be.

When she offers him the full-time position, he'll be both glad and relieved. Never having worked closely with her to begin with, Rex will probably become even more independent in his work habits, rarely if ever seeking her advice. At times, this will bother her. But she set the tone for their relationship from the beginning.

REVIEWING THE SALESPERSON

Salespeople learn a tremendous amount during their first three months on the job. New hires barely able to get through an online product demonstration in week three, run a credible demonstration by week nine. They may have stumbled and fumbled with customer questions in the early going. Now they answers those same questions comfortably.

As exciting as it can be to watch a new salesperson develop into a confident professional, the reverse can be true as well. Two months into their training period, new hires may still be giving a halting, awkward product demonstration. They might still be struggling to answer a frequently asked question in a relaxed and articu-

All salespeople, regardless of their experience level, need to be met with and have their sales performance reviewed on a regular basis. For the new hire, it's critical. Both good and bad work habits need to be discussed from the beginning.

late manner. Even in those early weeks, there could be some conflicts with co-workers.

No matter where they are in this continuum, the new hires' progress needs to be addressed at recurring intervals. Some small business owners might neglect to do this. Many don't understand the importance of communicating with new salespeople frequently during their early tenure. Others aren't sure what to discuss. Not formally addressing the new hires' progress on a frequent basis can lead to salespeople experiencing a number of different problems such as:

- Having an inflated opinion of their abilities
- Feeling unfairly criticized
- Being unsure of where they stand

INFLATED OPINIONS

Companies of all sizes experience difficulties when trying to hire good salespeople. When business executives feel positive about a new sales representative's performance, they may be thrilled about making a successful hire. With the best of intentions, they may keep any discussions totally positive, worrying that negative talk will cause the new hire to seek employment elsewhere.

This can leave new salespeople with the impression that they are stronger than they are. A misperception like this might lead to a cocky attitude and blown sales down the line. Even if their initial performance has been impressive, they cannot possibly be perfect. By not discussing areas in which they could improve or challenging them with another set of goals, a manager could be inadvertently stopping them from reaching their full potential.

CRITICISM ONLY

Some small business owners do make an effort to observe new sales representatives in a variety of selling situations. In the process, they might notice a few things that these reps could do differently to enhance their overall selling style. They may have made the mistake in the past of not addressing problems early on in a salesperson's tenure and don't want it to happen again. So they sit down with the salesperson and discuss the areas in which they could improve. Afterward they notice that the salesperson seems a little different around the office, maybe slightly detached.

The reason: there was no balance to the discussion. All feedback focused exclusively on what the sales representative was doing wrong. No time at all was spent on the person's strong points. The salesperson might feel confused, shaken up, or even a little angry.

Business owners should critique salespeople. They frequently dipense good advice. Unfortunately, salespeople focus on the overall negativity and ignore much of it. A competent manager weighs in on both the plusses and minuses of a salesperson's performance.

UNSURE OF WHERE THEY STAND

Some company presidents have few discussions with the new hires, either positive or negative. When this happens sales representatives have ambivalent feelings about their value to the organization. Besides employing salespeople who wonder how they are perceived by the employer, there's another downside.

With no real guidance, new salespeople may begin to set their own schedules and formulate their own goals. Their ideas may not be in keeping with what you as a manager want them to accomplish. Once they start directing themselves, supervising them becomes problematic. This causes unnecessary friction between the parties.

I tell my clients that no tougher job exists than hiring a person for an open sales position. Everything—and I mean everything—must be done to ensure that communications with salespeople are balanced, upbeat, and frequent. Impactful and noteworthy discussions could mean the difference between watching a salesperson flourish and seeing this individual go to work for another employer.

LACK OF EXPERIENCE

Some people reading the last several paragraphs may think they sound condescending. After all, what kind of manager would neglect to sit down and meet with a direct report? Who would provide nothing but negative feedback? That's management 101.

Company presidents with direct reports in departments where they have more knowledge probably manage them well overall. They may speak with these employees on a regular basis and in a balanced manner.

When it comes to the direct management of salespeople, though, they may feel very much out of their depth. We've all been there, haven't we? If we're uncomfortable we sometimes do and say things that we wouldn't under ordinary circumstances. Not having done the job themselves and not knowing how to connect with someone in the sales profession, the president might avoid meeting with them altogether. Reviews go unwritten, conversations don't take place, and communications go badly in general.

So what's the big deal, you might ask. Alright, the salesperson doesn't get reviewed. Hasn't everyone had a manager who skipped or simply didn't give annual reviews? Doesn't everyone survive? Yes and yes. But we're talking about salespeople here. We're talking about someone responsible for producing revenue for the company and dealing with the mental fatigue that comes from rejection. Sales reps need effective communication at regular intervals. When that communication doesn't take place, two demoralizing situations can occur: the average performer or the surprise resignation.

The Average Performer

Average performers are easy to identify in most organizations. It's a frustrating situation for whoever manages them. Typically, there are high hopes for these sales representatives in the beginning. They learn the product, go on the requisite number of sales calls, and start closing sales. No particular friction with co-workers is evident at any point. Many managers choose to leave sales representatives like this alone, feeling that they are doing just fine.

After eight or nine months, these sales representatives still aren't much better than when they started. They aren't any worse.

They just aren't growing in the position. Several productive months might be followed by a bad month. They might alternate between performing right at or slightly below quota. Even after they are no longer the new hire, they continue on this way. Having never been held to any standards of performance, they are in no real fear of losing their job.

Instinctually, many presidents realize that the salesperson seems fairly content and could continue to produce at the current pace for a good long while. This leaves them feeling depressed and resentful. How did the new hire get so comfortable? Will this new saleperson really be celebrating his or her year anniversary with the company in a few short months? Is that a good thing?

The Surprise Resignation

In my practice, I've worked with countless company presidents who have pointed to empty cubicles and said something like, "They were here for three weeks and then abruptly left without any real explanation." Or "I gave them everything they asked for: a larger base salary and an upgrade on their laptop. Then they told me it just wasn't working out here. Quite frankly, I'm afraid to replace them just to have this happen all over again."

Resignations occur with all kinds of employees, but they are especially frequent in the world of sales. The reasons are many. Salespeople, especially those with a field sales job, have more freedom than most employees. They interact with decision-makers at other companies all the time. If these decision-makers are impressed by their sales skills, they may want to talk to them about opportunities at their own company.

When salespeople don't feel supported by their new manager or aren't sure how they're perceived within the new organization, they just might be willing to listen. It's easy for a sales representative to fit in a job interview between appointments.

When asked why they would consider leaving their current employer after such a short time, many simply state that the company is not in as good financial shape as they were led to believe.

Others say that the potential to earn commissions was greatly exaggerated. Whether these statements are valid or not, some managers with hiring authority take them at face value and offer the sales rep a position with their organization.

Secondly, many salespeople resign their position after a major disagreement over—you guessed it—commission. After they have been gone for a while, their former employers may have thought things through and realized they made a mistake. They may contact the ex-salesperson and attempt to work things out so that the rep will come back. Salespeople, especially really good ones, do return to their past employers on occasion.

Lastly, salespeople send out a lot of resumes when they're looking for a job. They may have interviewed for several positions and even turned down an offer or two to work for your company. Hiring managers often keep in touch with sales representatives they've interviewed to see how everything is working out in their new positions. If hiring managers learn that a salesperson is dissatisfied with the new employer, for whatever reason, they may offer the salesperson a job. Again, not unheard of.

IMPORTANCE OF PERFORMANCE REVIEWS

For all these reasons, as well as others I may not have thought of, business owners must conduct regular reviews with new hires. These reviews are of particular importance during their first business quarter with the organization.

Reviewing a new sales representative frequently may seem like a daunting task, especially for a president who has never done so before. When the templates for the reviews are written in advance and the salesperson knows the exercise will be taking place, the stress level goes down a bit. It becomes more an exercise in gathering all the pertinent information and then having a two-way dialog with the salesperson. Performance reviews involve work, to be sure. Being organized beforehand cuts down on any mad dashes to the finish line.

THE 30-DAY REVIEW

Arguably the trickiest of all reviews, the 30-day review takes place at a time when the salesperson may not have met with many customers, given a lot of product demonstrations, or closed any sales. For these and other reasons, many small business owners don't bother with them. The exercise seems pointless to them with so little to talk about. While I am empathetic toward their viewpoint, I need to underscore the importance of the 30-day review.

As a sales manager, you must reinforce the fact that there are expectations of the sales representatives in your organization. They will be held accountable, even in the early stages, for their performance. When business owners do take the time to put a 30-day review together, they express surprise at the amount of progress that has taken place during the first month. Most find plenty to talk about.

The language of a 30-day review should include words such as "the salesperson is making great progress toward" or and "I've noticed major improvement in." On the other hand, where accurate, it should include phrases such as "not as much as we'd like to see" or "could use more attention." Overall, presidents charged with managing the sales representatives should offer their full support as new hires work hard to become a permanent part of the sales team.

A potential template for a 30-day review for a salesperson like Rex might look like that shown in Figure 13-1 on pages 187–189.

An example of a completed review is shown in Figure 13-2 on pages 190–193.

Figure 13-1. 30-Day Review Template

Attendance						
Number of Workdays:			**Number of Absences:**			
Punctuality	1	2	3	4	5	N/A
Comments:						

Company Property						
Cubicle	1	2	3	4	5	N/A
Common Area	1	2	3	4	5	N/A
Cell Phone	1	2	3	4	5	N/A
Laptop	1	2	3	4	5	N/A
Company Car	1	2	3	4	5	N/A
Comments:						

Interpersonal Skills						
Co-workers	1	2	3	4	5	N/A
Customers						
Company A	1	2	3	4	5	N/A
Company B	1	2	3	4	5	N/A
Customer Service	1	2	3	4	5	N/A
Operations	1	2	3	4	5	N/A
Comments:						

Figure 13-1. 30-Day Review Template (continued)

Productivity

	Total	Quota	Difference +/−	% +/−
Prospecting Calls				
Conversation				
Appointments				
Product Demos				
Proposals				
Closed Sales				

Comments:

Sales Revenue

	Total	Quota	% +/−
Product A			
Product B			

Technology

Sales Software System	1	2	3	4	5	N/A
Product Demos						
Product A	1	2	3	4	5	N/A
Product B	1	2	3	4	5	N/A

Comments:

Figure 13-1. 30-Day Review Template (continued)

Product Knowledge						
Product A	1	2	3	4	5	N/A
Product B	1	2	3	4	5	N/A
Comments:						

Sales Skills						
Introduction	1	2	3	4	5	N/A
Qualifying Questions	1	2	3	4	5	N/A
Objections	1	2	3	4	5	N/A
Product Demos	1	2	3	4	5	N/A
Closing	1	2	3	4	5	N/A
Comments:						

General Skills						
Time Management	1	2	3	4	5	N/A
Territory Coverage	1	2	3	4	5	N/A
Written Commun.	1	2	3	4	5	N/A
Sales Contests	1	2	3	4	5	N/A
Comments:						

60 Day Objectives
• XXX
• XXX
• XXX

Figure 13-2. Sample 30-Day Review

Attendance						
Number of Workdays: 20			Number of Absences:		1	
Punctuality	1	2	3	4	**5**	N/A

Comments: With the exception of one absence for a sick child, attendance and punctuality have been excellent.

Company Property						
Cubicle	1	2	**3**	4	5	N/A
Common Area	1	2	3	**4**	5	N/A
Cell Phone	1	2	3	**4**	5	N/A
Laptop	1	2	3	**4**	5	N/A
Company Car	1	2	3	4	5	**N/A**

Comments: Generally orderly, Rex keeps his cubicle neat and is respectful of his co-workers in common areas. A better system for keeping track of the product information he has accumulated would be helpful. Right now it's disorganized and difficult for him to access. His cell phone and laptop are in good working order.

Interpsonal Skills						
Co-workers	1	2	3	**4**	5	N/A
Customers						
Company A	1	2	3	4	**5**	N/A
Company B	1	2	3	**4**	5	N/A
Customer Service	1	2	3	**4**	5	N/A
Operations	1	2	3	**4**	5	N/A

Comments: Both customer service and operations report that Rex worked hard to learn about their departments, showed interest in what they did, and returns all calls or messages left for him. His interactions with co-workers are respectful and pleasant. Company A and Company B had positive impressions of Rex from the first sales call. Company B did mention that he seemed nervous and that proved to be a little bit distracting.

Figure 13-2. Sample 30-Day Review (continued)

Productivity

	Total	Quota	Difference +/−	% +/−
Prospecting Calls	133	167	(34)	79%
Conversation	11	14	(3)	78%
Appointments	6	5	1	120%
Product Demos	3	4	(1)	75%
Proposals	1	2	(1)	50%
Closed Sales	0	1	(1)	0%

Comments: Some parts of the orientation process took longer than expected, leaving less time for making sales calls. When he did have the time, Rex was focused on making the calls. He was over quota on the number of appointments, which was very impressive. Only 50% of the time (six out of three) did those appointments convert to product demonstrations. We will work together on this during the next thirty days.

The one proposal generated by Rex was well put together and the client he sent it to has real interest in our product. No closed sales were expected during this first evaluation period.

Sales Revenue

	Total	Quota	% +/−
Product A	0	0	0
Product B	0	0	0

Technology

Sales Software System	1	2	3	**4**	5	N/A
Product Demos						
Product A	1	2	3	4	**5**	N/A
Product B	1	2	**3**	4	5	N/A

Comments: Consistent about populating the software program after every call, Rex's note section could use a little bit more detail. His demonstration of Product A is excellent and I feel comfortable letting him give the demonstration to any customer solo. Obviously much more comfortable with Product A, Rex is falling short of expectations on Product B. He needs to show more enthusiasm during the Product B demonstration.

Figure 13-2. Sample 30-Day Review (continued)

Product Knowledge

Product A	1	2	3	4	**5**	N/A
Product B	1	2	**3**	4	5	N/A

Comments: Relative to his tenure, Rex demonstrates good knowledge of Product A. But he needs to develop better knowledge of Product B and a greater understanding of which type of client is interested in Product A versus Product B. He should work with marketing and customer service to learn more about the differences between the two products.

Sales Skills

Introduction	1	2	3	**4**	5	N/A
Qualifying Questions	1	2	3	**4**	5	N/A
Objections	1	2	**3**	4	5	N/A
Product Demos	1	2	**3**	4	5	N/A
Closing	1	2	3	4	5	**N/A**

Comments: Rex follows the introductions in the sales manual word for word, resulting in a number of strong conversations and appointments. This is great to see. Once in front of the client, Rex can sometimes address their objections in a halting, nervous manner. I know he can easily improve this with practice. The opportunity to close a sale has not yet presented itself.

General Skills

Time Management	1	2	3	**4**	5	N/A
Territory Coverage	1	2	3	4	5	**N/A**
Written Commun.	1	2	3	**4**	5	N/A
Sales Contests	1	2	3	4	**5**	N/A

Comments: None of the delays and rescheduling that took place during Rex's first month of orientation were his responsibility. He was consistently where he was supposed to be and prepared for the task. In terms of written communication, he has followed the sales manual regarding e-mails, follow up notes, and proposals. On his first day, I told Rex that as soon as he spoke with 10 decision-makers, he would receive a gift certificate to a restaurant. His 10th conversation took place during Week 3 of the first 30 days. Congratulations, Rex. Enjoy your evening out.

Figure 13-2. Sample 30-Day Review (continued)

60 Day Objectives
• Achieve 100% of pro-rated productivity goals in all categories
• Improve conversion of appointments to product demo from 50% to 75%
• Add more detail to the notes section
• Gain a greater understanding of Product B
• Practice Objections
• Manage independent time effectively
• Sales Contest: First closed sale earns a gift certificate to your favorite bookstore

CONDUCTING A REVIEW

The president has evaluated Rex as it relates to his performance against the scaled-down productivity goals. His general sales ability, product knowledge, customer relations, and the ability to get along with others in the organization were carefully assessed, as well. In an effective 30-day review a president should also make note of the progress a new hire needs to make toward becoming a fully productive salesperson. This was accomplished in the 60-day objectives section.

Hopefully, the review templates were designed in advance and shown to prospective hires during the interview process. If not, move ahead anyway. Create the content for the reviews. Give new reps a copy at least one week in advance. Let them go through the process of researching their own productivity numbers (if possible) and rating their own level of proficiency in the areas where they'll be reviewed. Have new reps submit this self-review to you at least two days in advance of your formal meeting.

If at all possible, conduct any performance reviews in a neutral location like a conference room or even another colleague's office. In this way, the sales representative feels at less of a disadvantage.

I recommend that my clients set a realistic tone for the review by saying something like, "The review process can be a little awkward for both parties, no matter how hard we try. I feel a little nervous myself. My main objective here is to look at what you've accomplished and support you in getting to the next level. Let's try and be as relaxed as possible. I want you to succeed here."

Whenever I take the initiative and admit that I'm a little uneasy about this process myself, the look on people's faces is almost comical. Typically, their expression goes from shock to one of a more relaxed acknowledgment that neither the giver of the review nor the receiver really felt totally at ease. Why not just come out and say it? We're all human.

Go through the written review in its entirety, explaining various sections. Answer questions the new hire might have. I then suggest taking a look at the new hire's self-review, paying special attention to any lack of agreement in certain sections. When an area of discrepancy comes to light, I recommend that an argument be avoided. Don't try and convince each other of anything at this juncture, just hear each other's point of view.

Rarely have I ever changed a sales representative's evaluation solely because the person disagreed with me on a particular skill or behavior. But the fact that we're not in alignment has heightened my awareness of the situation. I typically advise clients to say, "Thanks for being candid about how you graded yourself in terms of your knowledge of the sales software program. We view it differently and I'm glad to know that. Let's meet in a few days and discuss this specific issue."

By handling the discrepancy in this manner, no one feels forced to back down or to prove themselves to be inarguably right. By isolating the skill or behavior and looking at it more closely, both parties come to a better understanding of what is being asked for. The situation usually improves. If it doesn't improve, as a manager you need to start assembling the appropriate documentation to back up your claims. Then revisit the problematic situation with new facts or figures.

FINAL THOUGHTS

After seeing their performance review, new hires should know precisely where they stand *for the moment*. In my sample 30-day review, the company president was positive about the new hire's overall performance. The president conveyed those feelings with specific compliments. Criticisms were clear and backed up with the facts. New hires should feel good about their accomplishments to date and fully supported in their efforts to improve.

When company presidents feel displeased with their new hires' performances, those feelings should be reflected in the reviews. New hires should understand *specifically why* their 30-day performance ranks well below the minimum expectations. They need to be aware that if their work doesn't improve drastically between the 30th and 60th day, they may be in danger of not being offered a full-time position.

Thirty days go by quickly. Whether new hires perform well or poorly, you don't want to go *another* 30 days or longer without communicating with them about their overall performance against expectations.

14

Conducting Performance Reviews: The 60-Day Review

NEW HIRES SPEND MUCH OF THEIR TIME DURING THE FIRST 30 DAYS amassing product knowledge, observing others do their work, and practicing their sales techniques. Days 31 to 60 will see the emphasis change from watching and learning to doing. The salesperson's actual performance against productivity numbers becomes critical.

Differences between the 30- and 60-day reviews include the addition of the Pipeline Report and the Sales Forecast sections as shown in Figures 14-1 and 14-2.

Figure 14-1. 60-Day Review Template

Attendance						
Number of Workdays:			Number of Absences:			
Punctuality	1	2	3	4	5	N/A
Comments:						

Figure 14-1. 60-Day Review Template (continued)

Company Property

Cubicle	1	2	3	4	5	N/A
Common Area	1	2	3	4	5	N/A
Cell Phone	1	2	3	4	5	N/A
Laptop	1	2	3	4	5	N/A
Company Car	1	2	3	4	5	N/A
Comments:						

Interpersonal Skills

Co-workers	1	2	3	4	5	N/A
Customers						
Company A	1	2	3	4	5	N/A
Company B	1	2	3	4	5	N/A
Customer Service	1	2	3	4	5	N/A
Operations	1	2	3	4	5	N/A
Comments:						

Productivity

	Total	Quota	Difference +/-	% +/-
Prospecting Calls				
Conversation				
Appointments				
Product Demos				
Proposals				
Closed Sales				
Comments:				

Figure 14-1. 60-Day Review Template (continued)

Pipeline Report (New to this report)

Phases	% of Accounts
Phase I	
Phase II	
Phase III	
Phase IV	
Phase V (New)	

Sales Forecast

	% of Accounts
30-Day	
60-Day	
00-Day	

Comments:

Sales Revenue

	Total	Quota	% +/--
Product A			
Product B			

Technology

Sales Software System	1	2	3	4	5	N/A
Product Demos						
Product A	1	2	3	4	5	N/A
Product B	1	2	3	4	5	N/A

Comments:

Product Knowledge

Product A	1	2	3	4	5	N/A
Product B	1	2	3	4	5	N/A

Figure 14-1. 60-Day Review Template (continued)

Comments:						

Sales Skills						
Introduction	1	2	3	4	5	N/A
Qualifying Questions	1	2	3	4	5	N/A
Objections	1	2	3	4	5	N/A
Product Demos	1	2	3	4	5	N/A
Closing	1	2	3	4	5	N/A
Comments:						

General Skills						
Time Management	1	2	3	4	5	N/A
Territory Coverage	1	2	3	4	5	N/A
Written Commun.	1	2	3	4	5	N/A
Sales Contests	1	2	3	4	5	N/A
Comments:						

60 Day Objectives
• XXX
• XXX
• XXX

The completed 60-day review might look like the review shown in Figure 14-2.

Figure 14-2. Sample 60-Day Review

Attendance						
Number of Workdays:			**Number of Absences:**			
Punctuality	1	2	3	4	**5**	N/A

Comments: There were no absences during this time period. Attendance and punctuality continue to be strong.

Company Property						
Cubicle	1	2	3	**4**	5	N/A
Common Area	1	2	3	**4**	5	N/A
Cell Phone	1	2	3	**4**	5	N/A
Laptop	1	2	3	**4**	5	N/A
Company Car	1	2	3	4	5	**N/A**

Comments: Acknowledging that his product information was disorganized, Rex grouped the pamphlets into categories and put everything in a three-ring binder. He also created separate folders on his computer for all electronic documents. These were big improvements. In all other ways he continues to be respectful of the common areas and company property assigned to him.

Interpersonal Skills						
Co-workers	1	2	3	**4**	5	N/A
Customers						
Company A	1	2	3	**4**	5	N/A
Company B	1	2	3	**4**	5	N/A
Customer Service	1	2	3	**4**	5	N/A
Operations	1	2	**3**	4	5	N/A

Comments: Both companies spoken to for this review had positive remarks about Rex's sales abilities. Co-workers in all departments enjoy working with him. Operations mentioned that they do not feel he is totally comfortable with filling out Contract C. We will work on that over the next 30 days.

Figure 14-2. Sample 60-Day Review (continued)

Productivity

	Total	Quota	Difference +/−	% +/−
Prospecting Calls	256	300	(44)	85%
Conversation	21	24	(3)	87%
Appointments	12	10	2	120%
Product Demos	8	7	1	114%
Proposals	4	5	(1)	80%
Closed Sales	2	2	0	100%

Comments: There was an improvement of 6% on prospecting calls and 9% on conversations during this second 30-day time period. Rex's conversion rate of conversations to appointments continues to be strong and the number of product demonstrations exceeds expectations. Proposals were slightly off and closed sales were on track. One of his goals was to improve the percentage of appointment to product demonstrations from 50% to 75%. His 12 appointments resulted in 8 product demonstrations (66%)—an improvement, but below the goal. Rex must be at 100% of quota for prospecting calls and conversations for the 90-day review.

Pipeline Report

Phases	% of Accounts
Phase I	20
Phase II	12
Phase III	8
Phase IV	4
Phase V	2

Comments: With the average sale being $27,000, 14 to 15 sales per quarter will be needed to reach the goal of $375,000 (27,000 x 15 = $405,000). Therefore, the number of accounts in the pipeline needs to be tripled for those goals to be achieved.

Figure 14-2. Sample 60-Day Review (continued)

Sales Forecast

	% of Accounts
30-Day	3
60-Day	3
00-Day	5

Comments: As with the Pipeline Report, Rex should triple these numbers. Much of the effort involved in increasing both sets of numbers will involve making 100% of the prospecting calls.

Sales Revenue

	# of Sales	Total	Quota	% +/−
Product A	1	$31,000	N/A	
Product B	1	$11,000	N/A	
Total	2	$42,000	N/A	

Comments: Rex's first sale to Company ABC was $4,000 greater than the average sale ($31,000 − $27,000 = $4,000). In addition he closed a sale with Product B. Congratulations on both counts, Rex! Great progress has been made in becoming more comfortable and conversant with Product B.

Technology

Sales Software System	1	2	3	**4**	5	N/A
Product Demos						
Product A	1	2	3	4	**5**	N/A
Product B	1	2	3	**4**	5	N/A

Comments: There was an improvement in the notes section of the CRM system. Rex provided more detail as suggested in the last review. His knowledge of Product A continues to be strong and his enthusiasm during the Product B demonstration improved considerably.

Figure 14-2. Sample 60-Day Review (continued)

Product Knowledge

Product A	1	2	3	4	**5**	N/A
Product B	1	2	3	**4**	5	N/A

Comments: Rex worked diligently with both marketing and customer service to get a better understanding of which customer buys Product A versus Product B and it certainly showed in the sale he made.

Sales Skills

Introduction	1	2	3	4	**5**	N/A
Qualifying Questions	1	2	3	4	**5**	N/A
Objections	1	2	3	**4**	5	N/A
Product Demos	1	2	3	**4**	5	N/A
Closing	1	2	3	**4**	5	N/A

Comments: Rex has really mastered his introduction and use of qualifying questions, which accounts for the number of appointments he set. He handles objections more fluidly. His product demonstrations have improved and he now has a solid understanding of Product B. In the case of both of his sales, Rex might have asked for the order a little bit sooner. Needing to make three to five sales per month (depending on the size of the sale), he should work on asking for the sale earlier on.

General Skills

Time Management	1	2	**3**	4	5	N/A
Territory Coverage	1	2	3	**4**	5	N/A
Written Commun.	1	2	3	**4**	5	N/A
Sales Contests	1	2	**3**	4	5	N/A

Comments: For the next 30 days, Rex must manage his time so that he is able to achieve 100% of the productivity requirements. Having concentrated on the major metropolitan areas in his three-state territory, he must now come up with a plan for calling into the second-tier cities. We will work together on this. Rex closed his first sale and received a gift certificate to his favorite local bookstore. Again, great job Rex.

Figure 14-2. Sample 60-Day Review (continued)

90-Day Objectives
• Be at 100% of productivity goals at the 90-day review period
• Meet weekly with president to review productivity goals
• Work with operations to improve accuracy on Contract C
• Triple the numbers in both Phase I of the pipeline and in the 90-Day segment of the sales forecast
• Ask for sale more promptly
• Come up with plan to call on second-tier cities
• **Sales Contest:** Be at 105% of productivity goals and win a gift certificate to the mall. Triple number of accounts in Phase I of pipeline for a gift certificate to a sporting goods store.

PERFORMANCE CRITERIA

Presidents need to consider each of the 30-day periods separately. They should think carefully about what gains are to be reasonably expected during all three phases. Sometimes sales representatives (and all other employees for that matter) will take a step backward in their progress or don't improve as much as anticipated. Often presidents will ignore this situation, hoping the new hire will see the problem and correct it over the next 30 days. This doesn't happen too often. Any decline in the rep's performance needs to be acknowledged and talked about.

As an example, in the General Skills section of the 30-day review, Rex was given a 4 for time management. It seems as if there were some unforeseen interruptions during his orientation, none of which were his fault. Rex dealt with the interruptions and was as productive as he could have been under the circumstances.

During the second 30 days, however, interruptions were not a factor. The company president felt that nothing happened to prevent Rex from achieving 100% of quota for productivity. He was given a 3 for time management in the 60-day review.

Rex received a strong score for time management in the first review and a not so strong score in that very same section for the second review. He was performing at a high level *relative to expectations* during the first 30 days but perhaps should have made more progress at the 60-day mark.

A second example involves Operations. Throughout the first 30 days, Rex might not have made a sale or had to do much in the way of paperwork. He received a strong mark for what was expected of him in that time period. Having made two sales during the 60 day period, he needed to fill out paperwork. He didn't seem to have a full understanding of Contract C. Therefore, his mark was lower for the 60-day review.

The next time Rex needs to deal with Contract C, there needs to be a plan in place to make sure he fills it out correctly. He should feel supported in this task. Telling him or any new sales representative to "do it right" the next time won't magically make it happen.

A salesperson may have done a great job and received a strong score in a certain category at the 30-day mark. Reps aren't owed that same strong score if they haven't improved enough during the second 30 days to warrant it.

THE SALESPERSON AT 60 DAYS

As president, you're fulfilling your duty and reviewing Rex at regular intervals. Especially if you've never gone through the evaluation process in quite this way, you may have mixed feelings about the entire project. It could be that you find the extra work of writing and delivering the reviews taxing. Having to sit in a conference room and tell a rep that they need to improve in certain areas may cause you some anxiety. You might wonder, as well, how the new hire feels about the whole idea of being evaluated every 30 days. It would only be natural.

Since Rex was hired for a 90-day probationary period, he probably doesn't feel totally comfortable yet in your organization. He may still be making mistakes and worrying that he'll be criticized for them. His days might be less consistent than he'd like. Frustration sets in at times. Not yet a full-fledged employee, he probably continues to exhibit some "best manners" behavior. Like you, he experiences anxiety just before and during the reviews.

But this probationary period and the accompanying reviews have many plus sides for him. Because you're communicating with him frequently and in a balanced manner, he feels certain that he's becoming the sales representative he was hired to be. Why? You've been clear with him on where he stands to date. If you were truly concerned about his progress, he would have known about it. Closing his first two sales and winning a couple of contests have boosted his confidence. In general, Rex feels hopeful and optimistic. Wouldn't it be great if all new hires felt this way 60 days into their tenure?

Try to remember that in reviewing him at regular intervals you are doing the right thing for the company and for Rex. When you realized that he didn't understand Product B as well as he understood Product A, you asked several members of your staff to get involved in helping him. His much improved knowledge of Product B will make it easier for him to achieve his sales quota going forward.

By holding him accountable and offering support at the same time, you and every one in your organization are working together to make sure he succeeds. All of you can take pride in Rex's achievements going forward.

15

Conducting Performance Reviews: The 90-Day Review

THE 30-DAY REVIEW CENTERS ON THE NEW HIRES' ABILITY TO ABSORB THE training material, follow schedules, respect company property, and interact well with co-workers. During the second 30 days, the focal point changes. New hires need to channel all he or she had learned into the beginnings of sales results.

Now Rex, our fictitious salesperson, has completed the final 30 days of the training period with his new company. How do the 60- and 90-day reviews differ? At the 90-day mark, he should perform at or above 90% of what would be expected of any of the full-time sales representatives on your staff. During those final 30 days a new sales hire should be walking, talking, acting, and most importantly of all, *delivering* like a tenured sales representative.

In the sample below, I make no major changes to the review. Any adjustments between the 60-day and 90-day reviews involve expectations. A completed review might look something like that shown in Figure 15-1 (pages 210–213).

Figure 15-1. Sample 90-Day Review

Attendance						
Number of Workdays: 20			**Number of Absences: 0**			
Punctuality	1	2	3	4	**5**	N/A
Comments: Attendance and punctuality continue to be strong.						

Company Property						
Cubicle	1	2	3	**4**	5	N/A
Common Area	1	2	3	**4**	5	N/A
Cell Phone	1	2	3	**4**	5	N/A
Laptop	1	2	3	**4**	5	N/A
Company Car	1	2	3	4	5	**N/A**
Comments: From the beginning, Rex has been respectful of the common areas and company property assigned to him.						

Interpersonal Skills						
Co-workers	1	2	3	**4**	5	N/A
Customers						
Company A	1	2	3	4	**5**	N/A
Company B	1	2	3	**4**	5	N/A
Customer Service	1	2	3	**4**	5	N/A
Operations	1	2	3	**4**	5	N/A
Comments: Rather than wait until a sale had been closed, Rex worked closely with operations to learn how to fill out Contract C correctly. A third round of companies viewed their sales call from Rex positively, with Company B being particularly impressed by his demonstration of Product A. His relationships with co-workers continue to be solid.						

Productivity				
	Total	**Quota**	**Difference +/−**	**% +/−**
Prospecting Calls	452	450	2	100%
Conversation	35	36	(1)	97%

Figure 15-1. Sample 90-Day Review (continued)

Productivity (continued)

	Total	Quota	Difference +/−	% +/−
Appointments	16	14	2	114%
Product Demos	11	11	0	100%
Proposals	8	7	1	114%
Closed Sales	5	3	1	166%

Comments: Rex realized a 15% improvement on prospecting calls and a 10% improvement on conversations with decision-makers. When he was at less than 25% for most of his goals after the first week, we started meeting every other day to discuss productivity. Through our discussions, Rex realized that he was not maximizing his morning prospecting time and worked to change this by taking only one break and not getting distracted by other activities. Appointments, demos, and proposals remain strong. Congratulations on the five closed sales.

Rex wanted to improve the percentage of conversations to demonstrations (12/8–60 days and 16/11–90 days). Since his appointments have always exceeded quota and the number of demos have been consistently on target, I felt that focusing on his prospecting efforts was more of a priority. We can work together on the appointment/demo conversion in the coming months.

Pipeline Report

Phases	% of Accounts
Phase I	68
Phase II	16
Phase III	11
Phase IV	8
Phase V	4

Comments: With a total of 68 accounts in Phase I, Rex surpassed his goal of 60 by 12%. In addition, he increased the number of accounts in every phase and closed five sales, four in Product A and one in Product B.

Sales Forecast

	% of Accounts
30-Day	6
60-Day	5
90-Day	23

Figure 15-1. Sample 90-Day Review (continued)

Sales Forecast (continued)

Comments: Rex's prospecting efforts resulted in a big increase in the number of accounts in his 90-day Forecast, which was great to see (from 5 to 23, for a gain of 18). Though he missed his goal of tripling every number by having only five accounts in the 60-day forecast, overall it was a strong effort. Together we will take a look at when and why accounts drop off between the 60th and 90th day.

Sales Revenue

	# of Sales	Avg. Sale	Quota	% +/−
Product A	4	$20,250	N/A	
Product B	1	$16,000	N/A	
Total	5	$97,000	N/A	

Comments: Proving that his first sale of Product B was no fluke, Rex closed another deal for $16,000 as well as closing four sales of Product A for a total of $81,000. New sales revenue of $97,000 represents a very strong performance overall.

Technology

Sales Software System	1	2	3	**4**	5	N/A
Product Demos						
Product A	1	2	3	4	**5**	N/A
Product B	1	2	3	4	**5**	N/A

Comments: Rex continues to use the sales software system consistently and correctly. I would like to see him get inventive with the sales information and start running some self-created reports. Demonstrations for both products are strong, with no noticeable difference between A and B at this point.

Product Knowledge

Product A	1	2	3	4	**5**	N/A
Product B	1	2	3	**4**	5	N/A

Comments: While still slightly more comfortable with Product A vs. Product B, Rex is well-versed in both products at this point in his tenure. We will focus on his knowledge of the competition going forward.

Figure 15-1. Sample 90-Day Review (continued)

Sales Skills

Introduction	1	2	3	4	**5**	N/A
Qualifying Questions	1	2	3	4	**5**	N/A
Objections	1	2	3	**4**	5	N/A
Product Demos	1	2	3	**4**	5	N/A
Closing	1	2	3	**4**	5	N/A

Comments: From his sales training and working with the other sales representatives Rex realized that he was not moving swiftly enough after the product demonstrations to forward the sale along. He was trying to reach the decision-maker by phone a day or two after the demonstration was complete instead of attempting a trial close or setting up a time to speak right then and there. Rex is concentrating on obtaining some kind of agreement to move to the next step at the conclusion of the product demo.

General Skills

Time Management	1	2	**3**	4	5	N/A
Territory Coverage	1	2	3	**4**	5	N/A
Written Commun.	1	2	3	**4**	5	N/A
Sales Contests	1	2	**3**	4	5	N/A

Comments: Rex independently researched current clients in second-tier cities in his territory and worked with marketing to compile a list of prospects in that same area. Though no sales have come from this exercise yet, they will in time. Rex was not able to capitalize on his gift certificate to the mall because he did not reach 105% of all his productivity goals. This was a disappointment. He did, however, more than triple his Phase I accounts and received a gift certificate to a sporting goods store.

He has learned that he needs to achieve his productivity numbers on a daily and weekly basis. As soon as he starts falling behind, it becomes more difficult to catch up.

Second Quarter Objectives

- Reach 100% of productivity numbers on a weekly basis
- Analyze appointment to demo ratio during the first month
- Create and run two reports on sales software system by the second month
- Work with marketing to study one of our top three competitors each month

LONG SALES CYCLE

Some might be asking at this point, "What should I do if the sales cycle at my company is *very long*—say nine months or more? How do I judge the new hire's progress?" In the case of an extended sales cycle, closed sales may not reflect the new hire's effectiveness during the first 90 days. But productivity numbers and the quantity of legitimate prospects in the pipeline most certainly would.

As a starting point, analyze the performance data of past sales representatives from the first three months of their tenure. Take a close look at how many accounts were in their separate pipeline stages. If no data like that exists, think about how many accounts salespeople should be actively working at the 90-day mark if they need to close their first sale in another six months.

New hires selling a product with a long sales cycle must be highly proficient at cold calling and following up on leads. They need to be consistently identifying and setting appointments with decision makers. Product demonstrations for a percentage of those decision-makers should follow with regularity. Deficiencies in one or all of these areas should cause a manager to question the rep's ability to close sales in another six months.

Salespeople who sell a product with a long sales cycle need very competent interviewing skills. They must be able to correctly identify the decision-maker(s), ask excellent open-ended questions, and come away with credible answers. It's incumbent on them to make the case to you as their manager that a potential sale has a strong probability of closing. How else can they or you jusify spending the next six months to a year using company resources to try and close the deal?

THE 90-DAY NEW HIRE

A tremendous amount of work has gone into the writing of all three reviews. As Rex's manager, you had to set goals, assemble data, speak with his co-workers and customers, and observe him during the work day. What do you know about Rex and what do you do with the information?

Let's start with what was learned about Rex. If I were his sales manager, I would have observed the following positive attributes:

- Likes and has an aptitude for sales
- Possesses solid people skills. Able to get along well with management, peers, and customers with few difficulties
- Feels comfortable with decision-makers
- Enjoys competition based on performances in sales contests
- Has strong product knowledge
- Holds sufficient technical skills for the position

Though I would find very few absolute negatives with Rex, there are some areas in which he could continue to improve:

- Time management
- Prospecting
- Closing

Bringing all factors into consideration, the great majority of business owners would find Rex to be a solid sales representative. Most would be pleased with their decision to hire him and comfortable making him an offer to stay with the company.

THEN VS. NOW

What's the difference between how you might feel about Rex versus other sales representatives you've hired in the past? Most probably, having made the effort to review his progress with him every month, *you know Rex* really well. Whether or not you choose to bring him on board as a full fledged salesperson, the decision won't be an emotional one. You won't cross your fingers behind your back and hope that he works out. You'll base your decision on fact and observation.

That's the good news. But one of the sobering realities of getting to know employees well before making them a job offer is that you're also fully aware of some of their flaws. Rex may always struggle with achieving his prospecting numbers. This will be true on day 91 and may still be just as true on day 901! You must monitor those numbers regularly and take action from time to time.

Sending him for additional training or hiring a sales coach to work with him on closing may be a necessity. As the business owner or president you'll need to take the initiative and get him the proper help where necessary. There's no magic to all of this.

The process of reviewing a sales representative every 30 days has come to a close. Going forward the reviews will be less frequent. A decision now needs to be made whether you make the salesperson an offer of full-time employment. With all the information you have at your disposal, you should feel confident and ready to make the final determination.

Part Four

The Next Phase

16

Offering the New Hire a Full-Time Position

Though he'd worked for several companies as a sales representative, this was Terrence's first experience being hired for a 90-day trial period. Gerald, the president, explained how the trial period worked during the interview process. He provided Terrence with sample copies of the performance reviews and told him they would take place every 30 days.

While the monthly review process did prove to be stressful, the whole orientation period was generally positive and well-organized. Gerald made certain that everyone in the company helped Terrence learn what he needed to know to succeed. Who could argue with that?

On day 91, right after they finished going over Terrence's 90-day review, Gerald smiled at him, shook his hand, and said something like, "You met all your goals. Congratulations. I'm glad. You worked hard. I would like to formally offer you a position as a full-time member of our sales team."

Terrence doesn't remember exactly what he said in response, but he knows that he did accept the position. After a handshake, followed by an awkward silence, he just walked out of Gerald's office and back to his cubicle. He isn't sure what he expected once he made it through the probationary period, but this certainly wasn't it. After all the formality of the past three months, the formal job offer seemed so casual.

He can't share his good news with his co-workers. They are all on the phone with customers, oblivious to his new status. He would like to celebrate this event or talk to someone. "Oh well," he thinks to himself," maybe moving from the trial period to full-time employee is kind of a non-event at this company." Terrence logs into the sales software system and begins to half-heartedly make prospecting calls. All day long he feels oddly disconnected from his new employer.

MAKING AN OFFER

GENERALLY, BUSINESS EXECUTIVES FEEL RELIEVED WHEN THE WHOLE review process comes to an end. They may have put other projects on hold or been staring at a stack of untouched papers for weeks. If the 90-day period has ended successfully and they are extending an offer of full-time employment to the new hire, they may be all the more anxious to "get back to normal."

This period marks a crossroads and a danger zone in terms of your ability to successfully manage the new hire and the sales staff going forward. "Getting back to normal" can in reality mean falling back into bad habits such as spending more time in other departments and less time with the sales staff. It might mean the return of thinking that salespeople should be totally self-sufficient. Especially after such a thorough training period, surely they won't need an appreciable amount of your time anymore, right?

By all means, congratulate yourself for making a successful hire and sticking to the 90-day plan. Take pleasure in getting a little of your time back. But don't offer new hires full-time sales positions and then let still relatively new employees just drift back to their cubicle.

If you do, you're letting an opportunity slip away from you. After formally offering new hires a full-time sales position, do something fun to acknowledge the hard work everyone at the company put in. Engage in a meaningful discussion about your expectations of them for the next 90 days.

MARK THE OCCASION

I believe in special gestures as a great way to mark the new hire's transition from a probationary employee to full-time salesperson. It need not be a giant extravaganza, though. New salespeople still have to prove themselves. They may not have sold a tremendous amount of product yet. Depending on the length of your company's sales cycle, they may not have sold anything at all. New salespeople still need a certain amount of help, guidance, and support going forward. In some ways, they're just beginning their tenure with your organization. No one can predict their future sales performance.

Your new full time employee has, to date, successfully accomplished what was expected during the 90-day trial period. This tells you that this individual has a strong chance of being successful within your organization and deserves some sort of recognition.

So how do you mark an occasion like this? Remember, you're creating a sales culture. You're setting goals, holding sales representatives accountable to them, and publicly acknowledging those reps who achieve them. Some motivating gestures might include:

- A handwritten letter congratulating them on completing the 90-day orientation with your organization. Mention specific accomplishments that you observed during this period.
- A formal announcement at the sales staff meeting. Include bagels and coffee or bring in lunch as a special treat.
- Phone calls from a few executives at your organization to congratulate the new salesperson.
- A lunch with you and one other employee from another department who they felt really helped them during the orientation process.

When you hire remote salespeople, remember to do something for them, too. Their geographical location shouldn't prevent you from acknowledging their successful completion of the first 90 days. You might:

- Put the whole staff on speakerphone during a sales meeting and have everyone shout their congratulations.

- Send them a gift certificate to a favorite coffee shop.
- Write a personalized note.
- Have others within your organization give them a call.

Just don't forget about the remote sales representatives. As I've said many times throughout the book, they will remember and greatly appreciate any thoughtful gestures.

TERMINATION

Once the 90-day training period ends, the business executive can go one of two ways with the decision making-process: offer the salesperson a full-time position, or terminate the rep for lack of performance.

If new hires see that they're not coming close to achieving their orientation period sales goals, they will often leave on their own. However, some do stay through the entire 90 days in spite of a less-than-optimal performance. Maybe they think that the business executive will give them another chance. Perhaps they never really believed they'd be held accountable. They may not have another job to go to yet. Whatever the situation may be, they did not meet their goals and have to be terminated.

This unfortunate outcome discourages many business executives. After all the work that has been put into orientation, it all comes down to this? What was the point? Why not just go back to the old method of hiring the best available candidate and waiting to see what happened? Though not what you wanted optimally, you need to look at this termination as a victory of sorts.

Goals and milestones were set with the idea that if new hires couldn't achieve them initially, there would be little chance of them being successful with your organization going forward. Their inability to meet the scaled down goals tells you that they would be marginal performers at best. You've been there before. You wanted to avoid being stuck with another mediocre salesperson. You've accomplished that goal.

Should you decide to terminate new hires, make the conversation brief. They have been with your company for a very short time.

They were hired with the understanding that they had to prove themselves before being offered a full-time position. Have all your documentation with you and say something like:

> In reviewing your performance over the last 90 days, I have decided not to make you a full-time offer. I think you would be better off pursuing opportunities with other organizations. Today will be your last day.

Some new hires may be shocked, some may not. They may argue or leave quietly. It's hard to predict what will happen. Guiding you about what to do is easier: stick to the facts and then repeat your decision. A dialog might go something like this:

Salesperson: I know I didn't meet all of my goals, but I have gotten better each month. I have an appointment with the Johnston Company on Monday. That could be a huge sale.

Manager: In three critical categories: prospecting calls, appointments, and product demonstrations, you've been unable to achieve greater than 80% of expectations. Despite all of the coaching we've given you, you're still having trouble conducting a mistake-free product demonstration. After thinking this over, I've decided not to offer you a full-time position. My decision is final. Today will be your last day.

> **With any termination,** consult your human resources department (if you have one) or an attorney for specific advice.

Some new hires will continue to plead their case. Others may not. You may want to restate your position one more time, or you may not. If you do, refer to their performance statistics and reiterate that you will not be changing your mind about their employment status.

ON THE FENCE

Ideally, the decision should be simple. If new hires fail to achieve the goals set for them, they should be terminated. Sometimes, though, you are just plain conflicted about whether to terminate or retain a new salesperson after the trial period has ended.

What if new hires have solid product knowledge or a pleasant way with customers, yet experience trouble filling up their sales forecast? Did they easily meet prospecting and appointment goals, while falling consistently short of the required number of webinars?

Discuss these inconsistencies with the new hires and those employees involved in the orientation process. You may feel strongly they'll begin to meet and exceed all their productivity goals soon. It might take them just a little bit more time than other reps. Everything else points to their ability to be successful with your organization.

But if you're not going to terminate them and you are not 100% convinced by their initial 90-day performance, do you just offer them a full-time position and hope for the best? No, you don't.

Approach the situation a little differently. Rather than make new hires in this situation a full-time offer, extend their orientation period. However, I wouldn't have it last more than one or two months at a maximum. Avoid extending the offer for three additional months. That's another full business quarter, and everyone needs to move forward one way or another.

When speaking with the new hires about your decision to extend their orientation period, be clear about why you're hesitant to offer them a full-time position. Cite the specific criteria you're basing your decision on.

Depending on the situation, you may want to stay with the goals from the orientation period or give them a new set of goals for the next month or two. In either case, the goals should be written down and signed off on by both parties. Tell new hires that they must meet 100% of the new productivity goals during the extension period, without exception, or they will be terminated.

For some new hires the pressure will be too much and they'll begin to look for another job, even while still in your employ. Others will bear down and do everything they can to achieve their goals. If you're correct and they just needed a little more time to

A word of caution to business executives: Be certain that new hires merit the extra effort involved in extending the orientation period. If they haven't achieved 100% of their goals, you'll have to look into the reasons for it and potentially provide the additional training and/or coaching. If they weren't able to achieve the initial reduced goals, ask yourself if they'll ever be a top or even a consistent producer at your company? What are the odds?

fully meet the job requirements, you have saved yourself and the company the painful process of starting the hiring process all over again. If your gamble doesn't pay off, you must honor your word and terminate them.

SET EXPECTATIONS

Returning to a more positive scenario, once the decision has been made to offer new hires a full-time sales position, how do you avoid falling back into the same old habits of not spending enough time with them? How can you foster a less intense but still solid relationship with your newly minted sales representative? Much of it revolves around setting expectations for the next 90 days and sticking to those plans.

First and foremost, let new hires know that you'll continue to meet with them every month, one-on-one, during the next business quarter. Assure them that this will not be a formal *review*, just a monthly meeting. I recommend that both parties set the dates and times for all three of those meetings right then and there.

I advise my clients to schedule the meetings on dates that occur after the monthly numbers are in and any relevant sales reports are run. By planning these meetings in advance, you're committing to the new hires and giving them a better feel for how the new post-orientation relationship with you will be.

During these monthly one-on-one meetings, some or all of the following should be discussed:

- Productivity numbers

- Pipeline activity
- Sales forecast results
- Recent victories (strong product demos, closed sales, promising appointments)
- Recent problems (stalled contracts, difficulties with another employee)

When you get together with the new hires, ask questions such as, "How do you think everything is going? Any concerns? Can I or someone at the company be of help to you?" When asking open-ended questions such as these, you're keeping the dialog open between the two of you. By doing this, you continue to invest in their ongoing training and development.

In between those monthly meetings, I often advise my clients to schedule a short (10–15) meeting in the middle of the month. Just check in with the new hire. The tone of the meeting should be conversational and upbeat. Take a look at the salesperson's mid-month numbers and make a comment like, "I noticed you're more than halfway toward your prospecting goal with two weeks left to go. That's great. Tell me about some of those calls." Or "I understand that the Commerce Group was really stalling on signing their purchase and sales agreement. How did that work out?"

If you're seeing a persistent problem, it's all right to mention it during these brief meetings, but try and keep it conversational. You could say something like, "I've been noticing that you tend to be at only 30 to 40% of your appointment goal at the mid-month mark. Any thoughts on that?" Let the salesperson talk. See where he or she goes with it. The whole topic can be addressed more seriously during the monthly meeting.

CANDIDATE'S OPINION

You need to have a candid discussion with all new hires about their experiences during orientation. This is especially important if they are the first or one of the first salespeople that you put through it. These are some questions you might want to ask:

- What were some of the highlights of orientation?
- Which segments best prepared you for doing your job?
- Who was most helpful to you during orientation?
- Where would you like to have spent more time?
- Where would you like to have spent less time?
- Was there any segment of orientation that felt like a complete waste of time?
- What segments could I add that would be really helpful?

Be open to what they have to say. Don't be defensive. Take notes. If they are the first sales representative to be hired under the 90-day system, you're hearing only one person's opinion. Those reps motivated to succeed will understand what you were trying to achieve during the orientation process. Most will provide interesting and balanced feedback. It's another lost opportunity if you neglect to have this conversation.

MAKE A BET

Years ago, when I was a sales representative, the director of sales reviewed my annual goals with me. When we were finished he said, "If you meet these goals, I will take you out to lunch. If you miss these goals, you will take me out to lunch. Deal?" I agreed and we shook hands.

I thought this was one of the coolest motivational ideas I had ever come across. I really wanted this manager to take me out to lunch at the end of the year. Unfortunately, the company eliminated his position in a cost-cutting measure. The entire sales department, managers and salespeople alike, were really disappointed to miss out on the opportunity to continue working with this talented individual.

At the end of the year, even though he was happily employed with another organization, many salespeople at my company called to tell him whether they had won their lunch bet. He really enjoyed hearing from everyone and those conversations were a lot of fun for both parties. It was a tribute to his ability to motivate.

After you've gone over the 60-day review, announced the person's promotion at the staff meeting, and the two of you have discussed your expectations for the coming months, make some kind of a fun bet. It does not have to be identical to the bet the director of sales placed with me. Create your own. But make the effort. It's a great way to end the orientation period and begin the next phase of your relationship with the sales representative.

17

Completing Orientation and Moving Forward

Lucy enjoyed being in sales, but she had never liked working with Deirdre, the president. Deirdre had always made it clear through her actions (and non-actions), that she considered sales a necessary evil. A former CFO, She spent most of her time dealing with financial issues.

Then things began to change. Two salespeople resigned in the space of a month. One of them had only been with the company a matter of weeks. Lucy thought that the recent resignations would make Deirdre even more contemptuous of the sales department, but the opposite turned out to be true. She actually started spending more time in sales, not less. Lucy had heard through a contact of hers in marketing that the board of directors had been really tough on Deirdre during the last meeting. They were particularly critical of her management of the sales force.

Deirdre began holding sales staff meetings more regularly. During one meeting she asked the salespeople to tell her how they introduced themselves to prospects. She then asked everyone to e-mail their introduction to her. At another meeting, she brought up the topic of common customer objections. She made notes about each one the sales staff mentioned.

Lucy was surprised when Deirdre had a representative from their sales software program come in and give the staff some booster training. Though Lucy had always used the program, most of the salespeople did not. After a while, she could see that they were consistently putting in notes after each call. Lucy noticed several sales management books on Deirdre's desk. When she came in early one morning, Deirdre appeared to be having a meeting with some sort of coach.

The biggest surprise of all came when Deirdre didn't immediately replace the two sales representatives who had recently resigned. In the past, new salespeople sort of appeared with no warning. This time around, Deirdre announced in a staff meeting that she was beginning the process of searching for new sales representatives. She added that she wanted to involve the current staff in the selection of the two individuals. Lucy was astonished when Deirdre met with her one-on-one and asked for her opinions on how to make the interview process a success.

Once the new salespeople were hired, Lucy noticed that Deirdre really made an effort to help them get acclimated to the company. The new reps had a schedule to follow for the first several weeks. They spent at least some time in virtually every department. Lucy, who often got stuck training any new reps, was especially glad to see others being asked to share some of the responsibility.

Out of nowhere, Deirdre announced that there would be a sales contest for the tenured sales staff. Anyone who exceeded their monthly revenue goal by 5% would receive a gift certificate to the nearby mall. Was Lucy dreaming?

Once the new salespeople had been in place for a while, Lucy walked by Deirdre's office one day and saw that she was very absorbed by a spreadsheet on her computer screen. Deirdre said with a laugh, "Now that the two new sales representatives are hired, I can spend more time doing what I do best." In a hesitant voice she then said, "Can I help you with anything, Lucy?"

Deirdre involved Lucy in the interview process, for which she was grateful. She learned a lot and had begun to think about the possibility of managing salespeople herself one day. During their many meetings, Deirdre had let her guard down a little bit and they had gotten to know each other better. Lucy discovered that Deirdre was an interesting person with a phenomenal memory for customers' historical sales revenue figures. Not surprising, Lucy realized, for some one with a background in finance.

She sincerely hoped that Deirdre wouldn't drift back to her old ways of burying herself in numbers and having little to do with the sales staff. If that did prove to be the case, Lucy wasn't sure she wanted to stay with the company. She had already seen what life was like with very little management.

WHEN THE HIRING PROCESS WAS COMPLETE, LUCY AND DEIRDRE KNEW EACH other better. They held one another in higher regard. Always a strong sales representative, Lucy now has some interest in sales management. She knows that as soon as the company starts generating enough sales revenue to justify it, Deirdre would gladly give up any sales responsibility and hire a dedicated sales manager.

Deirdre could benefit from continuing to work more closely with a strong senior sales representative like Lucy. She needs an advocate on the sales staff. In turn, Lucy would learn a lot from being mentored by an executive as accomplished as Deirdre. Deirdre might offer the position of sales manager to Lucy one day. If Deirdre buries herself in spreadsheets and Lucy leaves the company, that will never come to pass.

CHANGING RELATIONSHIPS

If you've followed some or all of the recommendations in this book, you've spent a great deal of time and effort on the sales force—more than you were comfortable with or perhaps ever thought possible. Maybe you became a better time manager or just let a lot of work pile up. Possibly you learned to delegate projects or give more responsibilities to others in your organization. Whatever was true about your work style before you read this book, you inevitably had to make a few changes to accomplish everything.

Now much of the work is complete. Sure, you will make adjustments where needed to the sales reports. You will add updates to the training binder and look into a new pre-employment assessment tool that a colleague recommended. These projects won't be completed all at once, though. None of them will involve the number of hours required to create an orientation program, for instance.

Be mindful. Both the new hire and your current sales staff are observing your every move. They have seen you make all of these changes. Some may have been skeptical about your ability to carry these projects through to completion. Others undoubtedly had a negative attitude about any change at all. A few reps might be pleased and feel hopeful with all of the new attention being paid to sales. No matter how they felt, they are waiting to see how you deal with sales going forward.

Post-new hire orientation, business executives need to have a plan for the next phase of their involvement with the sales department. The plan needs to be realistic and specific, with completion dates attached to all initiatives.

This is your moment of truth with the sales organization. Believe it. You're entering a new stage. If you simply say to yourself, "I know now that I have to spend a consistent percentage of my time managing the sales staff. I'll be sure and do that," it won't be nearly good enough. Slipping back into your old patterns will undoubtedly be the result.

A Different Relationship with the New Hire

Once you offer new hires a permanent position in your sales organization, your relationship with them will change. They had little to no say-so with regard to their own time during the orientation period. Undoubtedly they knew that failure to adhere to the schedule would not have held them in good stead when it came time for you to make a decision about their future. Now that they're full-time employees, you may see new facets to their personalities.

Feeling micro-managed during the orientation period, they might look forward to being "on their own." With the exception of the scheduled meetings, they may even avoid you a little. The reverse may be true, as well. It's possible that they don't want the new freedom (fear of failure, fear of responsibility). They might demand more of your time than you feel is reasonable given their recent promotion. You just can't be absolutely sure of their reaction to their new found freedom.

Consider another factor. They know (or have been told) that the sales staff was managed more loosely in the past. Held to strict standards during orientation, new hires might see others in the sales department as "getting away with" more than they have been able to. New hires may be diligently working on their sales forecast, for instance, only to see that the salesperson one cubicle over never turns one in. Feeling as if they're being held to a different norm than the rest of the sales staff may cause them to feel some resentment.

If you suspect that this might be the case, have a candid conversation with any new hires. Acknowledge some of the lax management in the past. Talk about initiatives that you'll be working on with the current staff. Underscore, however, that no matter how they observe the others behaving, you expect them to adhere to the minimum standards outlined during orientation.

If you've never hired a salesperson for a 90-day trial period before, be prepared. Many business executives thought they knew the new hires well, only to watch in surprise as a new facet or two of their personality emerged once they were offered a permanent position. With reps no longer on their Sunday best behavior, changes will occur.

FUTURE INITIATIVES

New salespeople have had a lot to learn over the past three months, from how to load paper into the copier to memorizing the details of a new product line. Out of necessity you and others in the company kept a close watch on them during this period. That time has ended. You now understand the critical importance of continuing to meet with them on a regular basis. You may also wonder what you should be talking about during those meetings. What does the next phase involve?

Some topics to start covering could include:

- Time management
- Territory coverage
- Account penetration
- Increased product knowledge
- Product mix
- Sales plan

Time Management

You control new hires' time during their first few months with your company. Their time management skills may have been discussed during the interview process. You might have asked references they provided about their abilities in that area. But you really don't know firsthand how they'll manage their time now that they're on their own.

During the first few post-orientation meetings, ask them how they plan their time. See if this jibes with what you actually see them doing throughout the day. Make note if they sometimes appear directionless. Talk to others in the company about what they observe. Check their activity in the software system. Are there times during the day when you don't see any notes logged in? Share your thoughts and offer advice about the best way to manage their days and weeks over the coming months.

Territory Coverage

Yes, they know what area their geographic territory includes, how many accounts they have, and which accounts are the largest. They have probably been fairly busy making an attempt to at least introduce themselves to every account. But are they communicating with each account with the frequency that you would like? Do some homework before you meet with them.

If you have a software program that helps them plan their call rotation, see if they're using it. Check to make sure they're interacting with every account. Talk to them about accounts that may not have been contacted yet. Ask about customers that they seem to be speaking with overly frequently or geographic areas they are spending little time in. Get their perspective on how things are going. Assist them if they're struggling to keep a balance in their territory.

Increased Product Knowledge

New sales reps need to learn the basics of the product line so they can start selling. Over time, their product knowledge should deepen. Work with engineering and product development to gain a better understanding of what the new hire should know.

Perhaps employees from those departments could meet with new hires every month or so to help add to their knowledge base. Follow up with them after those meetings take place. Ask them what questions you should be asking the new rep to make sure they're retaining the additional knowledge. Their learning curve will be more subtle going forward, but new reps should continue to advance their product knowledge all the time.

Account Potential

Acme Distributors steadily increases their business with your company every year. Happily, there have been few service-related problems of any kind. However, only one of their many divisions buys from your company. You would like to see that change with Acme and a number of other accounts, as well.

Don't make the mistake of assuming that the new hires will instantly understand where all the untapped potential lies throughout their territory.

Begin to discuss your thoughts about the additional business opportunities in certain accounts. Draw up a game plan together. Brainstorm about what sort of assistance the rep might need. Getting into new departments or divisions takes time, preparation, and patience.

Product Mix

The Smythe Company, a medium sized account in the salesperson's territory, buys only one of your many products. Don't wait for the salesperson to discover this. Proactively discuss The Smythe Company and other accounts in the same position early on.

Before approaching any account about a product line expansion, the new hire must have a strong understanding of the account's needs and which competitors they buy from currently. Once the new rep knows the account well, discuss additional products he or she should suggest and how to present them.

Sales Plan

You want new hires to leverage the compensation program to their advantage and earn a high salary. But how will they do that? How many sales do they need to close and at what revenue level? How will they find enough accounts to hit their goals? What's their strategy for getting referrals? Working leads? Will they be joining any trade organizations? Are they reading trade publications? Are there brand new markets that they should be considering? How will they learn about this new market? All these topics should be part of the overall sales plan.

The sales plan, a sizable project, isn't written in a day. Neither you nor the new hire may have written one before. You may never have written one before. Put together a template for how you would like a sales plan to look, and work with the sales representative to complete it section by section.

Like the orientation schedule, no perfect sales plan exists. Just get started. Think it through logically. Create one that works for you and your organization.

THE CURRENT STAFF

Instead of hoping that things would change, you did something about the disappointing sales hires of the past. From accompanying new hires on sales calls with their largest accounts to the hours spent writing the sales toolkit, you did what needed to be done to offer them every chance of succeeding.

Rather than sit back and let them be responsible for their own sales achievements, you're making every effort to act as a real manager and mentor them. You're reading their sales reports and scheduling meetings with specific agendas on a regular basis. Yes, they hold the majority of the responsibility for how well they do with your organization. But you have a big say in it as well. You know that now.

Within your organization, one group of employees has the power to undermine all your hard work: the other salespeople. You need to put a plan in place to bring them up to the level of compliance that you're requiring of your new hire. Oddly enough, at this point, many or all of them will be *running behind* the new rep.

REALITY CHECK

Not every one of your salespeople welcomed the many changes that new hire orientation ushered in. They know that at least a few of these changes will eventually affect them. Some may have been hoping that many of your initiatives failed. They might be eager to see you go back to your old pre-orientation ways and ignore them.

Others on your staff, though not making as much money as they might like, are willing to accept a lesser income as a trade-off for the low stress, low accountability culture that existed previously. If you've hired people who weren't particularly money-motivated, they may not have any interest in changing their ways to increase their earning power.

A few people on your sales staff may accept and embrace the changes. Some may have disliked the lax environment and resented the lack of management attention. There are those who may be extremely envious of the attention lavished on the new hire and wonder why they weren't given the same treatment. Tenured sales representatives may see better management of the group as allowing them to earn more money. They might be willing to put in the extra effort to increase their income.

It's not always possible to predict who will act which way and why. Time will tell. You'll have to wait and observe. All of them will be on guard. No matter how the individual members of the tenured sales staff respond, you must now turn your attention to them. For the time being, leave orientation behind and shore up problems with the current salespeople.

ONE STEP AT A TIME

Credibility comes into question when any manager tries to initiate too many changes at once. Staff members know that some projects will get more attention than others. A percentage of them will fall by the wayside. They simply wait the business executive out.

Avoid this altogether by sitting down and talking to the staff. Explain what you would like to accomplish. Let them know they'll be involved in some of the projects. Attach time frames to each initiative.

Potential projects might include:

- Policies and procedures manual
- Job descriptions

- Sales plans
- Annual/quarterly reviews
- Career development

I recommend that my clients begin with the policies and procedures manual or the job descriptions. Involving current staff members on those two projects is easy. Presidents get a chance to see how the group works together. At the end, they'll know who participates, who sits back, and which sales reps bring negativity to the process.

Policies and Procedures Manual

Compensation plans generally cover the financial rules governing the sales department. Other issues need to be addressed and might be different from some general company policies.

Does anyone on your sales staff complain a lot about rules? Could there be someone who has a more rigid sense of "fair play" than others in the group? Those individuals might be good candidates to involve in this project.

Some topics might include:

- Vacation
- Phone coverage
- Customer service responsibility
- Lunch hour
- Expense accounts
- Reimbursable expenditures
- Travel
- Customer gifts
- Dress code
- Trade shows

Many of my clients express surprise at the number of grievances that get aired when reps participate in the drafting of the policies and procedures. They wrongly assumed that the staff was reasonably happy with how the department was run. The exercise of drafting the document serves as an unexpected reality check. Being given the chance to have some say over departmental rules often has a positive effect on the sales staff.

Job Descriptions

Does someone on your staff have good writing skills? Is there a particular rep you consider to be the "model" for everyone else? These salespeople might be the type whose aid you would like to enlist for this project. The job description should include:

- General responsibilities
- Customer(s)
- Market(s)
- Skill sets
- Sales reporting requirements
- Software usage
- Territory coverage

Start out by having one or more sales reps track how they spend their time for several days in a row. Ask them to write down every job responsibility they think they have. How does that compare to what you think they should be doing? Make your own list. For more good ideas, look at your own and other company's want ads for sales positions. In what ways are yours the same or different? With all this information, an accurate job description will start to come together.

> **Written job descriptions assist managers in doing their job more effectively, especially when the time comes to promote, issue a salary increase review, or put a sales representative on warning.**

Sales Plans

Among your current sales staff, some may have experience with a sales plan and others may not. The more ambitious among them might have written one for themselves. If management has been less structured and they're used to working day-to-day, many won't see the need for one.

There will be those who ask how a sales plan differs from being required to send out a certain number of proposals each week. Explain that minimum performance standards help break down larger goals into achievable units and keep sales reps focused. The sales plan deals with how and where they meet the decision-makers who might be interested in those proposals.

Start the discussion with your staff about what you think should be included in a comprehensive sales plan. Some suggestions might be:

- Lead development
- Vertical market coverage
- Trade show attendance
- Membership in professional organizations
- Industry gatherings
- E-networking

Similar to researching the competition, many reps enjoy working on a project like the sales plan.

Quarterly Reviews

I recommend completing a few projects successfully before taking on this initiative. Conducting quarterly reviews may not have been part of the management of the sales staff at your company previously. Your current staff knows that a review process makes them more accountable for their sales efforts and it will make them uncomfortable.

Meet with your salespeople monthly and go over their sales productivity, but conduct a performance review on a quarterly basis. Reviewing a salesperson only one time per year is insufficient. If too much time elapses between reviews and the salespeople are in jeopardy of not achieving their sales goals, it may be way too late to help them.

Luckily, you can use the new hire reviews as a template for the tenured staff's reviews. You may want to do some editing to make the review more appropriate for the senior members, but most of the hard work will have been done.

Sections that you may want to add to the tenured staff's review could include:

- Decision-making
- Problem-solving
- Account management

- Territory coverage
- Quality of work
- Training/development
- Career goals (annual only)

Involve your current staff when creating the reviews. Many of my clients question the wisdom of this. They wonder if the reps will offer much in the way of good ideas for a document that will judge their performance. If your staff knows you're serious about this, they will step up and offer solid suggestions. You'll be surprised.

Career Development

In the past, you may have avoided talk of a career discussion with the sales representatives. Maybe you felt the company was too small to offer them any kind of realistic upward opportunity. In part, this was probably a smart decision. No good comes from discussing promotions that may never materialize. It's a morale killer for sure.

The amount of sales revenue generated at your company might not allow you to promote anyone into a sales management position, for example. That doesn't mean you can't offer top performing reps promotions with accompanying raises and titles.

Such examples could include:

- National account sales representative
- Key account sales representative
- Senior sales representative

Even if you can't offer them the *exact* position they are looking for, you might be able to create a hybrid position they would find challenging. Salespeople interested in becoming sales managers might jump at the chance to be a selling sales manager. To gain experience, they would be willing to take on both revenue and management responsibilities. Another rep interested in sales training might lead the group in sales skills exercises during a staff meeting.

Be creative. Find out what their long-term goals are. Helping them achieve those goals—at least in part—may increase the number of years they stay with your company.

INVOLVING EVERYONE

In my experience, having too many sales representatives work on any one project causes problems. Ask only one or two to be in charge of each initiative. Some staff members may want to have a say in the outcome of all of them. That's fine. Let whoever is interested take a look at all the working documents. Listen to any suggestions or comments they may have. Just because they aren't heading up a particular initiative, doesn't mean they can't add value.

Not all of the tenured sales representatives will be happy with all the new projects taking place. Some may resent having to work on a sales plan, while others are downright concerned about being reviewed every quarter.

Involving the staff allows them to feel that they had some control and say-so over each and every initiative. Nothing was done without everyone's full knowledge. That's a positive and empowering way to start off.

18

Creating a Sales Culture

After their interview, the president walks Gretchen through the sales department. He shows her where she'll be sitting if she's selected to fill the open sales position. On the wall, she notices a large bar graph. The president tells her he puts a new one up every week so the reps can see their performance against quota for the month. Gretchen observes one rep's bar out in front of all the others.

On the opposite wall, she sees a picture of a popular local area restaurant surrounded by fake dollar bills. The president smiles and says, "As soon as we hit $150,000 in booked sales for our new product, we'll all go out to lunch. The sales staff voted on the restaurant. I'm looking forward to it. I love the food there."

As he's showing her out, the president hands her the most recent copy of a sales magazine. "We subscribe to this and for some reason, we received a few extra copies. Please take one with you." She thanked him and turned to go.

Gretchen hopes the president offers her the sales position. She can see her name on that bar chart. If she gets up to speed soon enough, maybe she can contribute at least one sale toward the $150,000 goal and go to lunch with the whole staff. He said he'd make a decision by the end of the week and give her a call one way or the other. She'll have her cell phone with her at all times until then.

WHEN THE PRESIDENT GAVE GRETCHEN A TOUR OF THE SALES DEPARTMENT, she observed a pro-sales environment. A current of energy ran through the whole area. She could picture herself making quota and winning prizes. She wanted to be part of the sales team the president had put together.

Gretchen is one of several strong candidates for the open position. The president finds himself in the enviable position of being able to choose among them. That wasn't always the case. In the past, considering himself an "accidental" or "temporary" sales manager, he spent little time with the salespeople. The low productivity reflected his lack of effort.

One day he realized that he could have a much bigger impact on sales and began to learn everything he could about managing the department. It took time and hard work, but he finally assembled a driven, motivated sales team and created a sales culture.

SALES CULTURE

How the organization as a whole views the sales department and the position of sales representative significantly impacts sales culture. Other notable determinants of sales culture include the:

- Office environment
- Sales personnel
- Business executive
- Other departments

NEGATIVE SALES CULTURE

In a negative sales environment, the following may take place:

- Non-sales employees get away with making detrimental remarks about individual salespeople and the sales department in general.
- Funding for other departments takes precedence over sales.
- Company executives fail to consider the sales department's interests when making major company decisions.

POSITIVE SALES CULTURE

When a company maintains a pro-sales environment, it translates into:

- Salespeople receiving the support, training, and tools needed to succeed
- Co-workers respecting the position of sales representative
- Open communication existing among the different departments
- Non-sales executives taking the sales department's objectives into consideration when making company wide decisions

OFFICE ENVIRONMENT

People visiting a company with a sales organization should be able to tell where the salespeople sit. The department typically has a look unlike any other. In a true sales environment:

- Motivational posters adorn the walls
- Sales results are posted for all to see
- Letters of congratulation are displayed in cubicles
- The salesperson of the month has a jar full of candy on her desk
- Copies of several sales magazines lie open on desktops

SALES PERSONNEL

Though sales reps attend staff meetings together and enjoy participating in group contests from time to time, it would be a mistake to call sales a team sport. Sales resembles golf more than say, basketball. For that reason, presidents creating a strong sales culture promote a team spirit but manage individual players. That includes salespeople who:

- Feel recognized and valued for their unique contributions to the sales effort
- Know their strengths and weaknesses
- Take action to address their weaknesses
- Work to further improve their strengths
- Enjoy one-on-one time with the president

- Understand that failure to achieve quota may result in their being put on warning
- Appreciate the importance of and willingly participate in ongoing sales training

BUSINESS EXECUTIVE

I've talked a lot in this book about the fact that your lack of experience with or disinterest in sales has probably kept you from spending a lot of time in that particular department. I understand, though, that you have a real passion for *your business.*

You may immerse yourself in trade journals, for instance, or serve on the board of directors of any number of industry groups. You might happily be the first one in the office every morning.

Going forward, you need to take *some* of the passion you have for your business and bring it into sales. A company president serious about creating a sales culture should be:

- Reading a book on sales or sales management several times per year
- Monitoring progress made regarding each sales representative's weaknesses
- Offering salespeople advanced training in their areas of strength
- Recognizing salespeople's accomplishments
- Meeting with sales staff on regular basis
- Developing a relationship with each sales representative
- Asking about and acknowledging the sales representatives' career ambitions
- Placing non-performing sales representatives on probabtion

To sustain the sales culture you've worked so hard to create you need to:

- Be aware of your own sales management strengths and weaknesses
- Attend sales management training courses
- Meet with peers to exchange ideas about the sales force

OTHER DEPARTMENTS

Sometimes my clients worry that creating a pro-sales culture will come at the expense of the other departments. Will they have to take away from marketing or product development? How will this look? How will the other employees feel about this?

I reassure my clients that the development of a functional sales group does not impact other departments negatively. The ability to be more present for sales without being less present for another department does take maturity and reflection, however. Be honest. Do you:

- Spend a disproportionate amount of time in other departments?
- "Help" very capable staff members with projects they could easily do themselves?
- Resist handing over responsibilities to others?

Ask and answer these questions. The exercise will help you let others in the company realize some autonomy and free you up to spend more time in sales without creating resentment among the other departments.

IN CONCLUSION

Earlier in the book, we established that you may not be the very best candidate to manage the sales department. Your true interests and talent lie elsewhere. You may long for the day when you can either hire someone to manage the sales force or ask one of your sales representatives to take over some of the duties. What I want to say and what I want this book to say is that it's OK to feel that way.

But for today and for the foreseeable future, you are the sales manager. That may not be your official title, but to the sales organization, no matter how large or small in size, that's who you are. They and the rest of the company are count on you to lead the sales organization.

You can do this job. No "secret society" of sales managers exists. Excellent training and reading materials are available for any executive who has the motivation and interest. With focus and discipline you are more than capable of effectively manage the sales force.

Thank you for sharing your time with me and reading this book. I hope that it has given you the confidence to take your sales force to a higher level. Please contact me with your comments and questions through my website: **www.accidentalsalesmanager.com**. I look forward to hearing from you.

Glossary

account penetration: Working with an account to ensure that it buys as many products or services as possible

assessment (pre-employment): A measure of a job applicant's abilities across a broad range of sales tasks; one method of determining strengths and weaknesses

bonus: Amount paid to a salesperson over and above the base salary, typically based on attainment of specific revenue objectives

call frequency: The number of times a customer should be contacted by a sales representative over a given period

close: Bring a sale to a successful conclusion through the negotiation of the terms and conditions, resulting in a finalized agreement to do business

cold call: Either by phone or in person, sales representatives' attempts to introduce themslevls and the company to someone they have never met or spoken to before.

contract expiration: A report listing accounts whose contracts are due to terminate

commission: A percentage of the total amount of a closed sale

commoditized product: A product available from a number of different suppliers. With few differences in the features or quality between suppliers, the product is often purchased exclusively based on price

compensation plan: The formal document under which a salesperson is paid a base salary plus commission and/or bonus

culture (pro-sales): Formal and informal rules, customs, and traditions within the sales organization that encourage and celebrate sales achievement and success

fact sheet (product or competitive): Descriptions and data about a business's product or service presented in an organized and easy to understand format

FAQs (frequently asked questions): Inquiries made on a regular basis about a product or service

field sales representative: Sales representatives making in person sales calls in a specified vertical or geographic territory

geographic territory: One or more areas (state, county, country, postal code, etc.) assigned to a sales representative on an exclusive or (sometimes) non-exclusive basis for calling on clients and making sales

gross margin: Sales minus the cost of goods sold

gross profit: Surplus left after subtracting expenses

inside sales representative: A sales representative who conducts most sales business (prospecting to closing) over the telephone and Internet. Very few or no on-site customer visits take place

inventory turn: Rate at which a company sells its merchandise or stock

key (or major) accounts: A company of importance in the salesperson's territory, often contributing a disproportionately large amount of sales volume relative to other businesses

long range forecast: A report tracking prospects planning to buy anywhere from four months to two years in the future

marketing collateral: Pamphlets, brochures, and e-material show-casing the features and benefits of a product or service

mark-up: Expenses and targeted profit added to the cost of a product or service

objections: Concerns raised by a prospect or customer at different points in the sales cycle

outbound calls: Phone calls initiated by the sales representative to potential clients or current customers

overstocks: Surplus or extra product

performance review: A formal written evaluation of a salesperson's work for a specific period

phone interview: A meeting or discussion with an applicant for an open position that takes place over the telephone

pipeline: Prospects in different phases of the sales cycle being actively pursued for their business by a sales representative

product mix: The relative sales volume of the full range of products or services offered for sale by a company

productivity goals: A set of measurable sales objectives that a sales representative is expected to meet or exceed, typically over a set period

production schedule: The timetable for the manufacturing or assembling of product

proposal: A plan or document that organizes and summarizes the terms for one company to do business with another

prospect: A potential customer

qualifying questions: Inquiries that help salespeople determine whether a prospect might be able to use theirproduct or service and has the budget to make the purchase

quota: The salesperson's share of the overall company sales goal

RFP (request for proposal): A formal process in which a bid is submitted by one company to win another company's business

ROI (return on investment): The profit or non-tangible gains (time saved in production or improved look of product) realized after the original cost of the outlay for a new product or service is subtracted

sales contest: A competition with set timeframes and goals that rewards specific accomplishments

sales cycle: The typical length of time and steps that it takes to close a sale

sales forecast: A salesperson's prediction or best estimate of which sales will close within a specific time frame

sales revenue: Cash or other assets regularly coming into a business

sales plan: A program for systematically working a territory to achieve or exceed annual sales quota

sales toolkit: A manual offering information or instruction on a given company's sales practices and methodologies, as well as product and competitive data

shipment of goods: Report showing when product has or will be sent to a customer

shortages: Inadequate supply of product to satisfy customer demand

SPIF (sales performance incentive fund): A sales incentive that targets specific products or services for a limited time and pays a pre-determined dollar amount or percentage for each one sold. It is typically used to alter the product mix or introduce a new product.

sales training: Instruction intended to introduce sales concepts and improve sales skills and abilities

target earnings (compensation): Expected annual earnings for salepspeople achieving 100% of their goals, equal to salary plus commissions, plus bonus

tenure: Length or term of employment with a company

territory: A geographic area, industry, or other customer segment that is or can be assigned to a salesperson

territory coverage: Calling or attempting to call on all current and potential clients in a designated geographical or vertical area

tiered compensation plan: A layered payment structure where salespeople earns a larger percentage of commission or bonus when they sell more of a product or service

training salary: Temporary compensation plan designed for a sales representative's probationary period

trial close: An effort to determine a prospect's true level of interest in a product or service before attempting to formally close the sale

trial (probationary/training) period: Specified or finite amount of time that an employee works for a company before being offered a permanent position

vendors: Merchant, retailer, wholesaler, reseller or other entity offering products for sale in the marketplace

vertical territory: A territory limited to one or a few industries

vertical market: A specific industry such as banking

virtual sales representative (remote): Sales representatives whose territory and/or office space is separate from and/or not located near the headquarters of their employer

warning: Conversation with or written document from the manager notifying salespeople that their performance is below the company standards. Document typically outlines what needs to be done to make improvements and within what time frame.

Index

Index